WAKING UP

Making the Invisible Visible

BARBARA BENNETT

BARBARA BENNETT

Printed in the United States of America
First Printing 2021
First Edition 2021 ii

ISBN 9798511165424

10 9 8 7 6 5 4 3 2 1

Cover image by Ogsaint.

www.BarbaraBennett.net

What readers say about *Waking Up*

"Barbara Bennett has sincerely and successfully shared her unique, individual soul's journey through her new book: WAKING UP: Making the Invisible Visible. It will no doubt illuminate your own path and assist you to see what cannot easily be seen."

— Patricia Albere, Founder of the Evolutionary Collective. Bestselling author of *Evolutionary Relationships: Unleashing the Power of Mutual Awakening*

"Years ago, Thomas Hübl sent Barbara to me to help her ground herself. I remember her openness and courage to explore the depth of spaciousness. This book tells us about her journey of being very connected to the subtle field as she makes progress, and expands, while holding All in presence, space, and consciousness. This book would support people who are open to the astral world."

— Marcus Hirzig, Senior faculty member who has worked extensively with Thomas Hübl since 2002

"This book stands out as a leader by revealing actual experiences of a soul's journey over thirty years. It stands up to its name. It is unique, raw, wonderful and riveting."

— Jesse Stoner, author, *Full Steam Ahead! Unleash the Power of Vision in Your Work and Your Life*

"One gift in reading *Waking Up*, it gave me ways to witness, and sometimes experience, the invisible. Another pearl, this book shows Reality through the eyes of Hindsight at its finest."

— Charon Hunniford, spiritual finder

"Exposes the energy to unlock gifts, abilities, and knowingness that will transform us—from a separation, survival-based experience, to an interconnected abundant and prosperous world."

— Georgina Batchelor, Registered Psychologist

"Full of good tools to help one realize we are so much more than we believed. Beautifully explained, I found myself very supported in reading the last chapter, it was powerful. Thank you for writing your book. I want a copy on my bookshelf."

—- Rita, spiritual seeker

"I liked the tension in her book. I never knew if she were going to find herself or lose herself."

"Potent and evocative. Enables the reader to witness, and sometimes experience the invisible in action."

"Disperses fear. Invaluable to many of us with little experience of these invisible higher states."

"Classic example of a hero's journey. She dives into wounds. Helpers on all levels arrive. Transforms into the exquisite Beingness of everything. Delicious, courageous, and so beautifully described!"

FREE OFFER

"Shooting Star @ Lone Tree" by Feist, Michael | CC BY-NC-SA 2.0

Just to say thanks for buying my book,

I would like to give you a complimentary copy of

Signs of Waking Up

A Fun Checklist

To get your copy, go to:

www.BarbaraBennett.net/checklist

Table of Contents

Preface

This book is about *one* Soul's journey of discovery. It is a journey of making the invisible visible.

Early on, I just wanted to understand who I was, why I acted in certain ways.

I had no idea there was a greater Reality, no idea there was a Life Force leading the way.

In the beginning, I didn't even know that I was on a spiritual journey.

I didn't know that my own soul was trying to make higher, deeper "invisible" realms become alive, awake, and actually "visible" to me in everyday life.

Now, I realize this journey is about *The One Soul,* differentiated only by individual perspectives—known as "you" and "me."

Somehow this book has found its way into your hands.

So, I would like you to come and explore with me. My greatest wish is that you take from this book whatever is right for you, whatever speaks to your soul, whatever encourages you to wonder, question, explore, expand.

How to Read This Book

Here are a few points to help navigate the journey in *Waking Up: Making the Invisible Visible.*

You will be reading actual excerpts from my personal journals as they came to me from May 1991 to March 2021, when I received "the whisper" to write this book.

These original journal entries, and musings, form the backbone of my unfoldment.

Most entries are written in the present tense; this is because this is how information comes to me, raw, in present time.

Indented italic text indicates where my ego has taken a back seat, and higher dimensions are coming in directly.

For the most part, journal entries are sequential. They follow my journey through years of personality exploration, deep personal inquiry, and amazing explorations with mystical dimensions.

Excerpts include many years of experiencing raw and wonderful frequencies—listening to the mystical whisper, exploring deep emotional issues, discovering abilities in sacred mediumship, and most recently learning to live within a new world paradigm, which is currently blowing my mind, profoundly affecting the world, and my everyday Life.

With gratitude, I invite you, dear reader to come along with me on a wild ride that is raw, wonderful, and profound.

If you choose, let's embark on this journey together as we search for hidden parts of ourselves, release limitations, and allow Life's Mystery to have Its way. So, fasten your seat belts and let's go!

Chapter 1: The Beginning

Thirty years ago, I had no idea of what "waking up" meant. As a life-long atheist, I was resistant to the idea of spirituality. Wasn't interested. Didn't care. I was tough. I was sure of myself, in control. But today I find myself writing about the inner workings of an underlying Reality! What happened? Actually, in retrospect, my journey began many years ago.

My husband was out in the garden tilling the soil. He loves preparing the earth and will soon be planting rows of vegetable seeds. But I wondered what was happening when he came into the house, exhausted, and laid down on the bed. I went out to the garden and found his gardening gloves strewn on the ground; his shovel thrown down too, not like him. I go back to check if he's OK. "I'm all right," he replies, weakly; but I'm worried, although he has just had a physical, and was supposedly fine, this isn't right. "I think we should go to the emergency room," I say. "No, I'm fine," he replies. "I just need to rest." I call the doctor, "Take him to the emergency room," the doctor says. My husband walks unaided to the car.

Less than ten minutes into our trip, he collapses, loses consciousness, and falls over onto the dashboard. My heart stops. Blind emotion. Distraught, I pull to the side of the road, frantically pressing down hard on the blaring horn. I'm in shock. A car pulls up in front of me, a man comes to my window and asks if I need help. "My husband is having a heart attack," I blubber. He replies, "There's a fire station right up ahead. Pull in; they'll know what to do."

I'm on auto-pilot now. The fire station is just up ahead. I pull in, a fireman runs out, takes one look at the situation, pulls my husband down onto the ground, and calls for help. "We're having a class in CPR right now," he says. "Go to the emergency room." He instructs, "We will follow in the ambulance."

I'm now driving to the emergency room in a complete fog. He HAS to be alright. I mean what's the chance of someone immediately stopping to help me, and what's the chance of a fire station being nearby; this must be some kind of a sign.

I get to the emergency room way before the ambulance. And then I wait for over an hour as the doctors work on my husband. What's taking them so long? Is he going to be a vegetable? Oh, God help. Let him be OK. Please help.

Two hours later, they hand me his wallet, shoes and belt. Now I'm back home, utterly alone. My husband is dead.

Even though I've always been a strong, tough, independent person, my world falls apart. It seems as if a huge part of me has died along with him. I feel like I've been unplugged from the sun. He was my high school sweetheart; it had been love at first sight. For over thirty years, Hank had been my anchor, my best friend, my love. I would never be loved like this again.

◆ ◆ ◆

Again, and again, I am propelled into a deep, dark, bottomless pit, a hole, a wound. The mechanism that propels me into this pit feels sort of like an orgasm; but it ends in intense pain rather than pleasure. I realize that if I am to get out of the hole, and get better, I have to make myself dive into the wound and experience the pain over and over again. Never in my entire life have I experienced such intense annihilation; never even knew that level of intensity existed.

Strange things begin to happen. Covering my pain, I plunge back into my day job as corporate officer and pay more attention to my journal. I'm driven. Always have been, now is no different. I can do this. I have vision. I know where I want the organization to go, and I can take it there. I have the strength, power, and position. I can make the big boys cry, and occasionally do.

Chapter 2: Personality Days

One day in 1994, when I was plowing mightily along, a friend gave me a book on the Enneagram. The Enneagram is a personality typing system which charts nine core personality types; it also houses a deep spiritual component. The system describes each type from a low dysfunctional level to a high self-actualized level. As long as I can remember, I've always been interested in understanding my own behavior, and other people's too.

So, I do some reading. I take an Enneagram test. I discover I'm a flaming "8." The eight is called Leader, Challenger, or Asserter. I get the picture. At the highest level "8," think Martin Luther King; at the lowest level think of the guy in the jungle who got all those people to drink the poison cool aid. Yow, I better be careful. That's when I start doing workshops with Don Riso and Russ Hudson, authors of the book.

Now I'm observing my behavior more closely every day. I'm learning more about myself. By observing my "8" pattern, I'm learning more than I did from all my years of self-refection, counseling degrees, and working with students, clients, and employees.

As a good "8," I'm applying what I learn. After all, theory is no good unless you can use it. See it in action. Change the world! I discover I'm trapped in an invisible prison. I'm being driven by my personality pattern. I'm not in control! Well, I can't stand it; I'll just make myself change. Yellow sticky notes go up everywhere at work: "listen," "pay attention," "don't try to convince others of your views," "use minimum force," "be sensitive to others' reactions." Sometimes I follow this sticky advice, sometimes I plow right ahead anyway. Damn! Control is such an illusion!

The Meeting

I'm still practicing. In the past few weeks, I think my personality pattern is beginning to soften a bit. Then one day, an opportunity: a big meeting is planned for the next morning. One of the officers is questioning the judgment of my staff and me. I am incensed! How dare he! Then I notice one of those damn yellow sticky notes and I know I have to try to approach this problem in a new way if I am to break my usual pattern. Normally, I'd retreat and plot the destruction of my enemy. This time I don't try to figure things out. I don't plot, and I don't plan. I know that my staff has made the correct decisions. I decide just to go in, listen, and allow things to unfold as they will.

For me, this meeting is a breakthrough. I keep my mind glued to the sticky note in front of me. I find that I can indeed just listen and observe! It's fascinating to watch all the ego personality wars flying by. My folks come through with flying colors, and I manage to hold my cool. In the end, my boss decides we have made the right decision. When the meeting ends, I know that all my practice in self-observation is beginning to have an effect. I give myself one "self-growth" brownie point. (This was before I knew I have such a long way to go.)

A Fish with a Coat

One day, while meditating, in my mind's eye a watery image appeared. I am like a brightly colored fish swimming deep within the ocean, my feathery fins are waving in warm currents. Somehow, I can see the "whole" of life, the "flow" of past, present, and future all around me. There are no barriers, no dams, and no place to hide. Up ahead an octopus is lying in wait and other sea creatures who would try to attack; but there are also beautiful beds of coral and forests of seaweed, rust, yellow and green, through which I pass. I see I have no control over these things. Life just unfolds. I sense that if I just stay within my own natural current, I give others and myself more peace. I don't need to be a personality fish running around saving all the other fish. I don't have to lead the whole damn school!

Yet later, as I ponder this experience, I realize I am not yet that colorful, free swimming fish. I'm more like a fish with a coat, the heavy coat of my personality. I need to continue to self-observe. I need to learn more about my own natural flow. I need to swim beyond my usual patterns. I need to allow my coat to dissolve thread by thread.

Lobster Girl Revealed

OMG, a huge load of information just came in, and it contains the entire "story," the underlying reason why I had countless dreams of a red lobster as a young girl! The dream was never scary, but I always wondered why. I remember chanting, "I love my mother. I love my father," over and over as I soothed myself to sleep. (This was probably a projection of what I wished to have from my parents but found missing.)

> *Then, BAM, I become the lobster experience: It's my fortification, the bastion, the defensive stronghold for my little self! I see it is red and silently powerful. Inside I can hide, defend, and be protected. Out in front, I have feelers that can sense all around, and I have powerful claws that can catch and destroy. My tail is armored, flexible, so it is able to swat anything that approaches from the rear. Wow, this is the perfect hideout, the perfect living enclosure for safety and security. Within this fort, I can move throughout my environment without much worry or fear of being attacked, rejected, or abandoned. I can just hole up inside. No one knew, not even me!*

Taking My Ego to Tea

As I continue to journal and learn more about myself, I decide to take my ego self to tea:

Me: Please, come in and have some tea. I've been watching you lately in a more deep and subtle way. So, I thought we could have a chat. I would like to get to know you better.

Ego: Don't know about the deep part. I'm a pretty superficial guy.

Me: Yes, but I just want to ask how your job's been going.

Ego: Well, I must say that it's becoming more difficult. I've been working hard all these years to keep you solid, and to reconstruct you again and again and again.

Me: And why is that?

Ego: Because it's my job. Don't you get it! I need to keep you in my box. I need to keep you under my spell. And now that you've asked, I do have something to say. It used to be so easy; you had no idea that I was ever here. Now you are seeing lobsters and having all these subtle experiences and learning about all this spiritual crap. It's enough to drive me crazy. I used to be able to get you to latch onto everything I did. Now, even when I send in a flotilla of thoughts, emotions, sensations, history, karma, conditioning—the works—you still don't believe me sometimes. This is a drag. It's tiring. And I'm getting fed up.

Me: I see. Oh, wait, suddenly in this moment something is morphing—it's Being, Consciousness, interacting with itself. There is no separate you. Ego decomposes, disintegrates, and disappears. This is simply another arising.

Ego: See, this is exactly what I hate. And I'm quite nervous. I'm supposed to be the one in control, dominating, in charge. I'm getting tired and worn out. Maybe I need rehabilitation, or job training, or something like that. How can I come up in a more functional way?

Me: Let's talk. More tea?

Ego: Yes, please.

Working with all this ego and Enneagram stuff just brings more and more weird, unusual experiences.

Above My Ceiling

I don't really know what's going on. This is all new territory for me. There is both wonder and fear. I'm listening to a meditation, but only intermittently do I hear the words. There is an exquisite sense of delicacy, a precise sense of my present experience. There is also an incredibly blissful divinity. And all this while I am very physically grounded.

I listen to the underlying space which says, "Come in. Welcome." It beckons me to "Leave everything behind. Give up. Join us."

It feels like there are aware, formless, invisible "beings" present—awake and alive. I can sense "their" presence and the desire for good in the physical world. There is also a faint sense of collusion.

They say, "You are one of us. Join our quest."

The bliss is overwhelming. What powerful perfume! It's irresistible, totally mesmerizing, engaging in a formless way. It feels like life existing within the most delicate of flowers. And there's also a peaceful "hub" of delicate, effortless motion. Brains and physical bodies do not exist and are not needed in this realm.

I question, "How can I be in this physical dimension and this elevated dimension at the same time?" And yet I know I can. I am. I have been here all along. Now the sense of other "beings" evaporates and there is just exquisite, precise blissfulness. What in the world is going on?

Holotropic Breathwork

I'm in an Enneagram Workshop with Don Riso and Russ Hudson. My first experience of truly opening up begins the night we are learning how to put ourselves into a light trance by breathing in a certain way. We are to be led through a guided fantasy. Right before the exercise starts, I hear someone say, "Allow the world to affect you." I was stunned. It had never dawned on me to let the world affect me. As an "8," I was always the one acting on the world and making things happen.

I have this "allow" thing in my mind as the preparation for the exercise starts.

But as it turns out, I never even hear a word of the guided fantasy that is designed to teach us how to breathe for the exercise to be held the next morning.

> *Instead, an incredible inner experience is unfolding. I notice a round circle containing my heart. It has a set of metal doors with tiny peg handles. It completely fills the cavity of my chest. The doors open slowly. I'm mesmerized, it's like a flower unfolding and my heart is exposed. Inside I see that my heart is beating very faintly, because it has been underutilized and is very weak. I know in this moment that my heart muscle needs to be exercised a lot more.*

Somehow this experience of my heart opening makes me cry. It's like I am in love. I am weeping tears that I had failed to shed over the years because I was too "tough." Little did I know that, again, this was only the beginning.

My life would never be the same after the next morning. I had no idea what Holotropic Breathwork meant; had never even heard the phrase before. Turned out it was pretty simple. Lie comfortably on the floor. Turn the lights down low. Breathe the way I had supposedly been taught the night before. Listen to loud music especially choreographed to lead one through the belly, heart and head "chakras" (don't know what these are either).

My exercise partner, Peter from South Africa, sits by my side to accompany me on my "journey." We've been instructed that all sorts of things could happen on our "trip." It could be like talking a psychedelic drug, but there were no drugs involved, only loud music and breathing. Like a good "8," I decide I would not be afraid of the experience. Instead, I say to myself, "Allow the world to act on me. Whatever happens, happens."

> I start breathing, and even before the music begins, I am off on my journey. I feel strange tremors running through my body. A thought enters my head, "Oh no, maybe I'm going to be reborn!" Relax. "Allow the world to act on you." I find myself crying, whispering to myself, "I wanted to do it softly, I wanted to do it softly." It feels as if my real-life birth had been too rough, too violent.

Instantly the tremors stop. (I guess I had already experienced my premature incubator birth the hard way). Gradually I lose sensation in my body piece by piece—arms, face, chest, head, and legs. The only thing I sense is white smoke and my mouth. "Oh God, just like an "8," can stop everything but the mouth."

What happens next amazes me. I am propelled into a universe I could never have imagined. And I am there totally.

I cease to exist in human form. I am in an infinite, glorious, world of luminous blackness. It is awesome. Timeless. This space is both Nothing and Everything, all at the same time. There is a sense of people dying and being born. There is no right, no wrong, no good, no evil. No pain. No emotion. This realm just is.

I remain in this world, this state, for almost two hours. I am incredulous, in awe. I'm feeling a direct kind of "knowing." And I know that many such "visions" are yet to come.

A Force Greater than Myself

I keep asking myself over and over "Who am I?" "Who am I?" And days later, as I close my eyes to meditate, I see something in the right corner of my mind's eye.

An incredibly powerful force is building and moving towards me. I am terrified! I know this is a force greater than I had ever conceived; and it could wipe me out in an instant. Yow, gigantic pieces of black and brown spheres are now heading towards me. And they are out to destroy. I am nothing, a speck, a piece of dust. My resistance automatically kicks in as the force races towards me. I'll resist. Stand tall. Then somehow, I just give in and say, "Go ahead, hit me, take me. I will allow whatever happens to happen. I give up."

*The rock-like force comes hurling towards me like a humongous hurricane. **I am prepared to be destroyed.** Then, miraculously, this awesome power passes right through me, leaving me intact, unhurt! **I realize what a ridiculous illusion my strong personality pattern has been.** There is no way I can control, or overpower, this force which is so much greater than myself. I cry bitterly. My personality pattern is a lie. My entire life has been a sham; strong, tough, independent, in control. What rubbish! I have failed miserably. I haven't been up to the task. I'm busted.*

But v-e-r-y slowly it dawns on me (I'm not an easy sell); **by failing with my personality pattern, I have actually won!** I know that somehow the power of the universe is indeed much, much, greater than myself.

♦ ♦ ♦

Later that night I sit outside under a cold wintry sky, again asking myself, "Who am I?" As I look up into the starry night, the wind picks up, and as I breathe, the world becomes ONE.

I am a spark in the luminous sky. The universe is all one piece, one giant fabric that contains everything. I am the same as the life force, the tree, a chair. I am the same manifestation, the same medium, as my mother, a fence post, a cat! For a few nanoseconds I experience Myself breathing myself!

Oh my God, I think, Now I've really gone off the deep end. I'm thinking like a yogi or something. But at the same time, I realize what I need to do. I need to find out more about this expansive new world that is being revealed.

Chapter 3: Deep Inquiry Days

How am I to learn about this new world that is being revealed? Oh, I remember my Enneagram teachers have a spiritual teacher who writes books. His name is A. H. Almaas. So, I go to a huge bookstore and ask; turns out they have one copy of one book by A. H. Almaas, *Diamond Heart: Book Two: The Freedom to Be*. I take it home.

I've been reading ever so slowly now for days. I'm elated. I'm reading about concepts and sensations and colors that I've already experienced! ***I am not crazy!*** I hadn't imagined it all. ***Other people experience the same kinds of things***! Whoa, this is tremendous reinforcement. I know I'm on the right path.

I keep buying books. I gorge. I read *Book One: Being and the Meaning of Life, and Book Three: Elements of the Real in Man*. Damn, this stuff is good. Another book, *Facets of Unity,* connects the nine Enneagram types, which I already know about, with nine "Holy Ideas"! In *Luminous Night's Journey*, the guy even experiences magic bubbles in the air! In pure awe, I'm learning about the hidden undercurrents of life. In pure gratitude, I'm experiencing the joy of discovery. I am so thankful to find writings that recognize the kinds of weird things that I sometimes experience. Reading, for me, is like being a kid in a candy store.

I'm beginning to experiment with the process I see embedded in these books. (As a typical "8" I have to do, move, act, and make things happen.)

The process seems to involve four steps:

1. Observe, non-judgmentally, everything that I do.

2. Allow myself to feel what is happening in my body (not easy for me who has successfully learned to cut off feelings).

3. See the mirror truth, as if I were looking into a mirror, with no interpretations.

4. Effortlessly explore what I see and then let it go.

Well, I'll give it a go.

Surprising Arisings

The process seems simple enough; but trying it is another matter. *The more refined my observations become, the more I'm amazed at what comes up*. One day I'm walking down the road, living in the moment, feeling really good. Then, all of a sudden, I notice that my mouth is dry. Mirror truth, panic sets in! I have no water. Where am I going to get water? This is not how it's supposed to be. I was having a nice walk. Now I'm all preoccupied, the fun is gone. I step back for a moment to observe like I'm supposed to do. I realize I'm reacting to the simple feeling of my mouth being dry; it's as if I might dehydrate and die! The reality is water is only minutes away, and I could actually live for days without it! Realizing this absurdity, I am able to "let go" of my panic and get back into rational mode. I have begun to realize how unconsciously I build upon simple mirror reflections, adding more and more layers of things conjured up from the past.

Another time, I'm getting ready to do my morning exercises and get a call from friends who are going to drop by. Observation: I'm pissed. I don't know why, but all I can feel is tenseness and anger. Mirror truth: I want to do what I want to do when I want to do it. Well, I then attempt to effortlessly explore. Screw the mirror truth! I'm still pissed. I can't let this one go.

A third time I'm in bed thinking about what my mother told me happened when I was about six months old. My mother, lonely and overwhelmed, visits my competitive, hard-charging father who is away at officer training school. Mom finds out that dad had a "girlfriend." Now the weird morphing that happens to me, happens again.

Suddenly I find myself morphing into a timeless dimension and I become my six-month-old infant self. I'm lying in the middle of a double bed. My parents are in turmoil. A terrible sense of sadness is in my body. I close my eyes and follow the feeling. The sadness grows and fills my whole Being. It changes into a painful blackness, like a huge black hole. The hole grows larger and larger. I'm feeling love, desire, radiating out from every pore in my body. But nobody notices! I want to be picked up, held. No one cares! My emerging love is not recognized. Both parents, young and emotionally immature, are completely enmeshed in their own relationship troubles.

From Pasta to Volcano in the Pool

I continue to have my observation realizations while visiting Peter, who is now my partner. But the underlying motivation of my personality pattern doesn't really come out until I'm standing in the middle of his pool in South Africa. The "process" begins simply enough in the house, when I become extremely upset because Peter is absurdly cooking pasta in a tiny little pan. I observe my emotional reaction. It's over the top, way out of proportion to the actual event. It's only pasta for God's sake!

But I can't shake my annoyance, so I follow it instead. It grows and grows. It changes into a big black hole of deficiency. Somehow, it seems like I have failed. I continue to watch the process. Anger turns into sadness. Sadness engulfs me. I allow big tears. I stay with my feelings. Then sadness turns into anger once again; by this time, I'm out by the pool, so I walk right in. Now, I'm standing in the middle of the pool with the sun blaring down on me. My anger grows and grows.

I lose sight of where I physically am. My innards turn into fire. I'm frightened but let the fire rage. Flames erupt and become a gigantic volcano spewing fire, molten rocks and lava all over the world. I'm absolutely enraged. I didn't want to adopt my angry personality pattern. I was just a little kid. All I wanted was to be noticed, loved. I wanted to be picked up and touched and cuddled.

I'm pissed because I had to turn "hard" to protect myself, to wall myself off from being hurt. I wanted to do it softly, but the world had screwed me. I had to give up my essence to get love, to please my parents, to be what they needed me to be at that time, a strong, independent kid who didn't make demands.

Now I want to burn up the entire world! The fire rages and then becomes less and less. Amazingly, the anger ceases, and in its place, arises a sense of calm, stillness, and a warm welcoming blackness. It's all good.

Wow, I want to learn more about this observation practice. This inquiry stuff is incredible. I'm astounded by all the experiences I'm having, but I'm also scared. I feel like I should have a teacher, or some kind of guide. I start to search. I find a little puny website and end up writing to the "webmaster." The webmaster calls me on the phone. I learn that A. H. Almaas is a pen name for Hameed Ali, who is the founder and leader of an international spiritual school called Diamond Heart. There are thousands of students who meet in various groups, on a monthly basis around the world. Their teachers have been trained in the "Diamond Approach" for many years. The students who join this school, belong to specific, long-term groups, which they affectionately call their Diamond Heart group. A person needs to qualify to join a group and become a student. And guess what, a new Diamond Heart group is going to start up in my area in only two weeks. Wow, I apply, hold my breath and am accepted.

My Diamond Heart Sessions Begin

My group's first workshop is on Basic Trust. It is taught by one of the Diamond Heart teachers. It's not unlike the

Enneagram workshops I had attended with Don and Russ, except here, the focus is on essence rather than ego.

After listening to the lectures and participating in the exercises, I realize that I actually lack basic trust. I don't trust my environment. Deep down, I believe I can only rely on myself. I have to take care of my own needs. I do not believe in the "natural flow" of the universe.

Through various workshop exercises, I learn how my present view of the world has come from early childhood experiences. I have developed into who I am because of characteristics that have been held, or reinforced, by my parents and society. My father would say, "Don't let anyone push you around." "Stand up for yourself." "Don't be a sissy." My mother would say the opposite, "Be kind." "All people are equal." My parents actually disagreed on everything, and I was in the middle.

My dad loved to play roughhouse with me and make my mother mad. In retrospect, I never knew if he really wanted to play with me or just make my mother angry. My father could be very loving one moment and threatening the next, yelling at me for bringing him the wrong screwdriver. These were the kinds of things that made me suspicious of life and not trust my father. I wanted to love my dad and have him be there for me. In reality, he stayed away much of the time. I learned I couldn't count on him.

◆ ◆ ◆

I keep questioning my identity. This morning, I awoke to a personal revelation, a deep knowing of some kind: ***I am NOT my personality pattern, character, or body. I am a Nothingness, which contains Everything!***

Wow, now I'm really out of my league. As I'm explaining what happened this morning to my Diamond Heart teacher, that I had lost all my boundaries to mind or body, he looks me right in the eye and says, "You're not actually the person you think you; there is a higher dimension of no-thing-ness that is coming through you." Those words hit me like a lightning bolt! In my heart I knew that he spoke the truth. But having a force greater than myself working within me was too much. It was unfathomable. I completely lose it and cry uncontrollably for a long time.

◆ ◆ ◆

When I return home from the Basic Trust workshop, I experience an extreme sense of lostness, which lasts for days. I send an email to the teacher: I need some guidance. I'm having a great deal of difficulty assimilating what happened at the workshop, and other, similar, experiences which I've been having for the past few years. At one point, you described such experiences, with which I thoroughly relate as *mystical*. I was floored! But it didn't really hit me until I got home.

Now I'm overwhelmed. I think I may be having some mystical experiences. As a lifelong atheist, this is unfathomable to me. How could this be? I didn't ask for this. And it seems this would have overwhelming implications for my life. Somehow it shakes the very ground upon which I walk, the house in which I live, and the friends in whom I confide. I receive nothing back from this teacher.

◆ ◆ ◆

Now, I'm scared out of my mind. I know that I have to work this out by myself, and I will. I think part of my dilemma is that underneath everything, I don't feel good enough, or strong enough, to have been granted such an immense privilege, although intellectually I have read that this access is each human's birthright. But those were just words, only a concept, until now. Now I can't seem to understand anything I see. Is that really a chair? What's a chair for? Is that the wind, or something that I can't even imagine? I need help!

♦ ♦ ♦

The next day my friend brings me a book called *Spiritual Emergency*. This book is a Godsend. It describes what I am going through! It helps me gain an expanded perspective and understand more. I realize that many people go through these types of experiences. It is all documented! I don't have to change my whole life! I settle down and continue my "processing" every day.

♦ ♦ ♦

Diamond Heart also assigns personal teachers for each student. I begin to work with my teacher over the phone. My personal processing is becoming even more intense. During my first phone session, I discover I'm blocking the hurt that I experienced when I was not seen by my parents as an infant. I felt that nobody would take care of me in the way that I wanted. I now see I'm resisting feelings of betrayal and helplessness. I see how I resist feelings of love, softness and tenderness, especially for myself. I realize I have invented a hidden process to deaden my pain. A gray dullness comes into my body, or I go up and experience a sense of transparency.

I discover these sensations are signals that I am resisting the deeper pain.

◆ ◆ ◆

This morning, my inner domain is flooded with gray. I let it be and follow it in my body:

My heart area is gray, dull, nothing, dead

I am invisible as a baby

HOW COULD THEY DO THIS TO ME?

I am helpless and defenseless

My entire body is very constricted, tight and hard

I'M WORTH MORE THAN THIS

Constriction tightens across my heart area

I can't breathe

An ALIVE, SPARKLING, ENERY FIELD ARISES

Allowing vision and understanding

I have an inner alarm system like a museum

This protects the precious gems

I feel deep, sharp, solid pain in my tailbone

An intense energy field covers up/encases/encloses

I feel a small hard pebble in my heart

◆ ◆ ◆

A month later, during my group's Diamond Heart session, I discover that underneath my pattern of strength, there is a tiny, vulnerable, worm-like area which hides behind a giant metal shield! This shield protects me. And it also cuts me off from life; this shield has been with me since childhood. Back then, my child-like strength was no match for the giant adults that surrounded me. So, I learned to be strong. I took care of myself and stayed out of the way. I rocked myself to sleep at night singing about love. Maybe I was trying to convince myself that my parents loved me.

After a telephone session with my Diamond Heart teacher, I realize that my entire ego life is a sham. I feel completely empty. There is nothing left in me, not a cell, or a trace, not even a whiff, whatever that means. "I" am "gone," blended into a world without boundaries and no method of navigation.

I notice how I become extremely frightened whenever I find myself in this no-boundary space. There are NO signposts, no manuals, nothing to even give a clue as to what to do. I'm completely vulnerable. If I move an inch, I feel I will fall into the never-ending blackness and disappear, cease to exist.

Triggers

This morning, I pulled a muscle in my back, not that badly, but it makes me react. I feel angry. I realize I'm pissed at the situation, the world, and the pain. I don't want pain again! I remember to "relax into" the pain.

My anger turns into incredible hurt. This anger is really a very deep hurt! My parents cut me off. The world cut me off from my own essence, my authentic self. I must not be worth anything. I experience intense worthlessness and more hurt. Now, I'm mad at how

I'm judging myself. I'm mad at my ego, at my superego. I'm mad that I am judging my judging! It is hopeless. I can't do this anymore. The truth is that I just want the pain to go away. I'm tired of the whole thing. I'm tired of trying to figure everything out, trying to get somewhere. I hate pain. I don't want to feel it. Wow, I realize that the pain in my back has triggered a whole world of pain coming from the past. I'm tired, broken. I give up.

◆ ◆ ◆

I spent 21 days in an incubator like this.

I'm contemplating. Suddenly, I notice a separate part of my self, set off in a corner.

I didn't even know this little-girl-self was there, never saw her before. But here she is, separate, sad and lonely. I realize that this little, skinny, blonde girl is still a part of me. It's a part that I have abandoned, rejected, didn't want to hear from.

I look at her and say, "I am truly sorry. It's OK now. I can see you. I know that you're here. I can accept you. You can come home now."

I feel an incredible softness, an exquisite tenderness. And this feeling is for "me," for this little girl who has been left out in the cold, cut off, trying to do it all alone.

I begin to think, again, of my incubator experience as a newborn.

Twenty-one days of isolation, alone in a metal incubator, the latest invention designed to simulate the womb. But no touching is allowed, fed by a tube, no mother to help me regulate, only an immature nervous system and the will to survive.

Instantly, I warp speed through time, propelled into my actual infant incubator experience.

Incubator Baby

Born premature, no eyelashes or fingernails

Placed in the newest of incubators

Metal box, metal lid, no windows, completely black

Waking Up

Nothing to touch, no blanket, no Mom

No touching allowed

Every so often the lid opens

Oh, too much light, noise, movement

My tiny body immediately contracts

Nervous system screams

This is it! This is it! Get it now. Only chance. Food! Survival!

The hole must be filled

Must have contact, something, anything

Tube enters, disturbing tender flesh

Liquid bypasses mouth

Something's not right, no sucking, no Mom

Liquid enters stomach, Oh, physical relief

Left alone again—like a piece of raw meat

The pain remains, doesn't get discharged. It sears the inside of my helpless baby soul. I'm left in the jangly bottomless hole.

Wow, I realize that being open allows me to warp speed into other time dimensions and experience old occurrences in present time.

◆ ◆ ◆

I remember growing up, and through my adult years, the thought of food is constantly lurking in the back of my mind. No matter where I am, or what I'm going, I'm thinking about where and when I'll be able to eat. Will food be available?

There's a kind of panic that sets in; I need to eat. I have to eat. Get out of my way! This phenomenon happens even when I am not physically hungry.

> *I begin to observe more carefully. I realize there is something deeper going on. I discover that I am unconsciously warp-speeding back into the incubator time and time again. Eating doesn't fill this underlying emptiness. There is unbearable aloneness. There is a circular pattern of wanting/needing to eat.*

Oh, forget this inquiry thing! I'm sick of it! I want something to just come "in" and settle me.

◆ ◆ ◆

I realize that **my daily practices of walking, contemplation, and meditation keep showing me things, whether I like it or not**. I realize how I keep a walled-off place to retreat to inside—to stop hurt, scared, and rejected feelings. I stuff the pain from both the inside and outside.

> *Warp speed, now there's a cotton cocoon in my soul that is impeding my "flow," my internal movement, freedom and aliveness. This area has been unseen, off limits, dead for a long time. My child-like ego believes this place has to <u>stay frozen</u> to keep from dying of emotional pain.*

But I realize that this is a very early embedded perception that is no longer true. And it's no longer a useful strategy.

Inquiry

Diamond Heart is big on the skill of inquiry. It's really not a big deal. You relax, "do nothing" and just observe what happens within you. You notice your thoughts, feelings, and sensations. You learn to "let them go" and pass like clouds in the sky.

This is easier said than done. I just keep wandering off or am "triggered" by things I cannot "let go."

But I want to become more skillful. I want to be able to experience myself more directly—to go inside and know more about who I really am at my center, underneath all the beliefs and identities that I've learned. I want to go inside and experience the truth in this very moment, real time. And this is what inquiry is designed to do—to go past initial impressions, see what gets me triggered, and discover how my sub-conscious mind is actually determining what happens in my everyday life—good or bad, high or low. I want to know more.

♦ ♦ ♦

I realize that I have learned to repress my true nature. When I was an infant, the world was like sensation soup. Everything was my direct experience. I was one with my surroundings, like it or not. I experienced my deeper nature directly, whether it was with complete comfort, love, joy, delicacy, vulnerability, helplessness, hunger, delight, warmth, or distress. I had no labels back then; I didn't know about things in the physical world. I had no barriers. I just *was*.

When I was growing up, my environment started to shape me; it started to reinforce me, like when I was seen as cute or smart or strong or busy or bright. Slowly I learned to cut myself off from my deeper reality. I began to pay way more attention to the outside world. My reality was hidden under layers and layers of learned beliefs. My ability to experience the full range of reality, of Life, got hijacked.

I want to learn how to go beyond my usual learned perceptions. I want to go into a deeper reality. I want to explore the truth. I want to stay in contact with my experience. I want to learn now to follow the thread of what comes up, like I did in the pool in South Africa. I want to practice exploring and navigating uncharted waters. I want to use inquiry as skill, a technology, to help me find my way. The ego part of me can't really know what's right. It can't see its own identifications.

In order to go deeper, I know that I have to become quiet, subtle, still. I will have to pay close attention if I want to discover the truth. I will have to be willing to suspend all my learned beliefs and go with what I am actually experiencing in real time. It's like one of my teachers says, "If you have a big red radish in your stomach, then you have a big red radish in your stomach." And that's what I'm going to do— whether I like what comes up or not.

Homework: Father Issues

I'm at yet another Diamond Heart retreat. For homework, I'm supposed to reflect on my relationship with my father. Diamond Heart says that how we feel about our father affects how we feel about God. Well, here goes nothing: I loved my father dearly as a kid. I couldn't wait to have him come home. He took me swimming and let me dive off his head. When we drove to the lumber yard on Saturdays, I sat really close to him and he put his hand on my knee, all comfortable like.

Oh brother, now I'm having flashbacks. When I'm about twelve-years-old, my Mom and Dad decide to get a divorce. One night, when I get up to go to the bathroom, I hear them talking in the next room. They are talking about my little brother and how Dad is going to visit. When they had finished their discussion, and were ready to leave, my Mom asked, "What about Barb?" Without hesitation, my father says, "I don't care about Barb, she's just like you." I'm devastated. I just crawl back to bed and cry and cry. He betrayed me. His "love" is, was, all a big fat lie.

An earlier flash back comes, I'm eleven years old and my brother is six. My father comes to the door and says to my mother, "I'm taking the kids." I freeze inside. My Mom says, "Where are you taking them? When will you be back?" My Dad doesn't answer.

We drive on back country roads. It's pitch black, no lights and hardly any cars. I crouch way down on the floor behind the front seat. I'm thinking that my father is going to drive off the road and kill us! I braced for the crash. (I feel sorry for my little brother who hasn't got a clue.)

After about twenty minutes, the car stops. Confusion. Bewilderment. There are very bright lights. We are at the local town fair! I don't know what's happening. I am not safe.

◆ ◆ ◆

Thank God I'm now in a safe place, no more morphing back into episodes with my father. So glad I'm now married, for the second time, to the friend who brought me the spiritual book that helped years ago. I am now in a safe, friendly, relationship, with someone who actually loves me.

Snickers Bar Emotion

Together, my husband and I have joined a different Diamond Heart Group. Currently we are at this retreat. I happen to be sitting on our bed in the motel, thoroughly enjoying a Snickers bar, which I only occasionally allow myself, or else I would become addicted. My sweet husband comes by and says, "Are you going to eat that whole thing?" Instantly, I am infuriated; I am so mad inside that I can't even speak. I think this is ridiculous; I know my reaction is over the top.

When I calm down a bit, I remember this great new book, *The Language of Emotions: What Your Feelings Are Trying to Tell You* by Karla McLaren. Well, I just happened to bring this book with me, so I'm going to look this baby up. I look up anger, page 167.

"Anger is for Protection and Restoration. It includes Rage, Fury, and the Healing of Trauma." Well, I guess this should cover it. The book suggests that I ask myself some questions, "What must be protected? What must be restored?"

OK, this calls for inquiry, always a useful tool. I go inside and explore. I remember the times at home, to which I most looked forward; those were the times I could eat. Eating wasn't allowed between meals, and because of my fast metabolism, I was often hungry. Now I was getting closer to the trigger for my over-reaction. I realized, there were leftover imprints in my nervous system from my incubator days, and my physical need to eat as a child. So, when my husband suggested that I should not be eating "the whole thing," which I was so thoroughly enjoying, I went bananas. It wasn't like I was overweight or eating a gallon of ice cream or a bag of cookies for heaven's sake. It was a tiny little Snickers bar.

I go back to McLaren's book. She tells me there are gifts to my anger, like honoring my own boundaries and having a healthy detachment. I love this book. I continue and follow her suggestions on how to honor my anger. She explains how to ground myself and define my boundaries. She suggests that I make a list of all the unconscious contracts I have made with myself. After I had completed my processing, I end up literally burning the papers on which I had listed all my unconscious contracts. This was a way to release my trapped emotions, and behaviors, which fostered my ongoing anger. Wow, this process is just like Diamond Heart.

I see how my old, buried patterns come back to trigger me time and time again. Each time this happens my feelings grow even more intense. *I notice that once I have processed the greater intensity, I am even more open to whatever wonders may unfold.*

The Universe Supports Me

My Diamond Heart teacher and I finally meet in person, this time at a week-long retreat. I tell her I need a cure. Lately, no matter how I inquire, I end up in the same place, near this huge black hole. I'm petrified and cannot make myself go in. My teacher asks, "Can you walk towards the hole?"

Instantly I envision a black empty sack in my abdomen and genital area. I'm in the hole like a flash. I don't fall, instead I experience waves and waves of incredible fear. My body trembles, I'm sweating like a pig, but my hands are ice cold. Finally, the waves of fear stop. I keep my eyes closed. My teacher asks me to look around and describe what I see.

*I'm floating. I'm suspended somehow. I'm back into the black, but it's a warm, black, luminous universe! I feel supported! I feel like a dark red piece of fruit that's suspended in yellow Jell-O. I'm feeling the support of the universe! I can't believe it. I press my shoulders and legs down to test this support. Is it really here? It is! I am made up of zillions of cells, which are filled with flowing energy. And **my energy is the very same energy-medium that makes up the entire universe!***

I'm amazed that a huge black hole can yield such universal support.

◆ ◆ ◆

At Diamond Heart Retreats, I am learning many concepts. Here are some of the basics to which I like to refer: Soul, Essence, and my own invention, the individual bubble of reality.

I learn that the **soul** is pure, living, plasma-like consciousness, which differentiates Itself in many different ways. The soul is impressionable and malleable, sort of like silly putty. It can pick up images and impressions, like the colored comics on Sundays. The soul serves as a conduit, through which personality flows, and is transformed. The soul includes both my ego and my higher self. And it is through this living *organ of perception* that we come to *know* about things that exist beyond our usual, limited, human perceptions. These are the things I want to know.

Essence is our deepest inherent nature. It is the ground, the very nature that underlies everything—you, me, the body, the brain, the physical universe, everything. I'm beginning to see how essence is the very nature of who I am, but my experience in this real time is fleeting, and I am often unconscious.

It is my deepest wish, my deepest desire, to become more conscious of this inherent, essential, underlying intelligence. We are all born with this natural quality, just watch a baby and you can tell. I've seen how *essence, when it is unhampered by ego, radiates out its pure aliveness, love, truth, and joy*. I can sense that the highest, deepest, part of me somehow guides my consciousness towards freedom from my chattering mind, towards liberation. And I want to be free.

But it dawns on me that *we are all like individual bubbles, individual globes, spheres of life suspended in the universe*. Each one of us develops our own unique ego/personality perspective, our own unique "moonscape." The outer part of my globe is crusty and hard, full of learned ridges and ruts. (I need to learn how to soften the crust.) The inner part is Essence, freedom.

But here's the rub. *I cut off my essence with my ego*. I allow the crusty parts of my personality to become so big that they block the natural flow of my soul. My ego patterns become so fixated, so intense, that I don't get to see, experience, or utilize the actual energy of my soul or the energy of my essential self. And, I have a sense that, unencumbered, essence of the soul is what changes us. Essence is the very dynamic, the chemistry of the bubble, in which I have learned to live.

Higher Dimensions Phooey!

This morning my mind is driving me crazy. It's running non-stop like ticker tape on Wall Street. What is this mind doing anyway, and what about the ego? Diamond Heart talks about ego structures, ego illusions, ego limitation, ego immaturity, and ego maturity.

The ego mind gets conditioned; this limits our perception and takes over the way we live and act in the world.

I look up ego in the dictionary. Ego: the self, the division of the psyche that is conscious, most immediately controls thought and behavior, most in touch with external reality. So, what's going on here? What am I actually doing? Am I just playing a role that I've learned?

OK, I'm going to experiment, I sit quietly and just watch. I'm going to see what my mind is up to. I'm going to stay in the present, in the "now" moment, like the books say.

Every few seconds I observe my mind wandering off. I think about the eggs I had for breakfast. My "to do" list pops up. I see how my mind constantly drifts into the past and the future. What about the now? This "now moment" is slippery; this is not easy.

OK, I stop. I empty my mind; but it won't be quiet. It just keeps producing content, even when I don't want it. It chatters and wanders and analyses and judges and prefers. It's constantly running an inner commentary, on every little thing. One tiny little thought, and that thought branches out into a whole story. I give up. I'm going to start breakfast.

Brushes with Death

Christine

Today I'm at the Hospice House. I have volunteered here for a number of years because, after reading *Autobiography of a Yogi,* I wanted to assist people who were dying in a way that gives them comfort and dignity.

I'm standing in the doorway of Christine's room; something has radically changed. I've known Christine for nearly six months. She's an isolated, crabby, old lady who is dying in bitterness. When I first met Christine, I was serving her breakfast. I asked, "Would you like me to come back and visit with you?" Her answer, "Well, I really don't care." I respond, "Well, I think I'll come back and bug you then." To tell the truth, over the months, we've sort of become friends. But this morning is different.

Her room has a warm, soft, glow and Christine is sitting up in bed.

I come in, "Christine, what's happened? You look so peaceful."

"Oh, that's the nicest thing anyone has ever said to me," she coos.

I'm amazed. I walk over and sit on her bed beside her. Now, I'm stunned. There is a liquid golden light streaming out from her eyes! How is this possible? I am overwhelmed. I start to cry.

Christine says to me, "Barbara, you are going to be all right and I am too."

A few days later, Christine died and I cried. She had taught me a great deal.

Peter

I'm in shock. Got a call from South Africa this morning, calling to tell me something about my Peter. "Are you sitting down? Sit down. Peter has been murdered. Thieves broke into his house last night. Edith found him this morning when she came in to work." I'm stunned. I can't really take this in. And I'm supposed to be traveling to a Diamond Heart retreat tomorrow.

◆ ◆ ◆

Well, I came to the retreat anyway, even though I'm still reeling. I can't get Peter out of my head. Don't quite know what I'm doing. I wake up at 5:00 AM. I'm crying. I sit on the edge of the bed, mourning Peter. I can't stand it; I'm in agony.

*All of a sudden something is pulsing in and out from a point, continuously, nano second by nano second. I watch. I'm mesmerized. And then I get the download. OMG, **LIFE is coming in and out of existence! This is how Life emerges**. I'm astounded. This is what is actually happening every second. Now I'm crying tears* *of Joy. Thank you, Peter for this lesson. It's the ones left behind that mourn, while the Truth is pure majesty. My world view becomes radiant, even the doorknob is pulsing. I am in bliss.*

Mom

I'm now helping my Mom hold a straw. She is in the process of dying. We are very close, head-to-head.

*All of a sudden, I warp speed into an unfamiliar dimension. I look down at what's happening. Mom and I no longer exist. **"Beingness" is just administrating to "Beingness."** Extraordinary! In this domain, Mom and I, on the physical level, are doing absolutely nothing. A greater power is taking care of things, having Its way.*

♦ ♦ ♦

Every day when I help Mom get to the bathroom, the same dimension is occurring, without her knowledge. She walks v-e-r-y slowly, and looks all around, as if she is seeing things for the very first time. When we get to the bathroom she says, "What do I do?"

"You just go into the bathroom and go to the bathroom."

"Oh," she replies.

I notice that this wondrous perspective only occurs on the way to the bathroom. It's when she reverts to her usual ego perspective that she becomes agitated and fearful.

She yells, "I just want to die. I want it to end."

"Mom, if I could help with that I would, but the dying process takes its own time. Each person is different."

"What do they do at the hospice house where you volunteer?"

"One thing is they teach people how to meditate"

"Well show me how," she says. (This is from a woman who consistently tells me that reading anything spiritual is a waste of time, and if I am still meditating, I am being "selfish.")

I give it a try anyway, "Just close your eyes, relax, and watch your breath."

She tries for thirty seconds and says, "Where is my breath?" She gets all flustered and barks "This is stupid." (I thank God for the bathroom trips.) Mom passes quietly in the night. I'm flooded with joy. Mom finally got her wish.

Past Life Regression

Diamond Heart Retreat Groups also break into smaller groups of eight to twelve people. In this way we can work on more personal issues with a small group teacher. I'm in such a small group meeting now at this week-long retreat. The teacher asks each of us to check in to see how we're doing. When she asks me, I suddenly begin to impulsively stamp my feet on the floor. I'm terrified. I tell the teacher that something bad is about to happen. She comes over and holds my hand and asks a student to do the same on the other side of me. I hardly notice. I've been transported into another frequency, way back in time.

I'm a man. I'm lying in a rickety wagon. I hear wooden wheels clacking on cobblestones. There are loud voices. My hair is all matted. I have a blousy kind of shirt on, which is all dirty and sweaty. My arms are stretched and chained by the wrists above my head. I am about to have my legs torn off.

Suddenly, a blood curling scream blasts out of me. But now I'm just watching, calmly thinking, "Oh, I guess there is going to be screaming; I hope I won't disturb the people in the other cabins." A second scream erupts. And then just silence. It's over, and I slowly come back into the present-day session.

◆ ◆ ◆

Back in my room, I am astounded, overwhelmed. This experience was not like I was just *thinking* about the incident or recalling it. My consciousness had time traveled to the original event. I was re-living the actual experience of being transported in the cart, hearing the sounds, smelling the smells. I could do nothing but watch and allow.

I'm still trying to recover from this past life experience. For days it continues to go around and around in my head. It's as if I have PTSD. My teacher tells me to just process it slowly and take my time.

Creating Collages Soothes Emotions

When we get home from the retreat, I begin to make some of my collages. The cutting and pasting and absent-mindedness help to relieve my jangled nervous system. I love putting the various shapes and colors together, and I come up with some of the weirdest designs.

Colors

Diamond Heart actually teaches about color. Often retreats are based on certain colors that may come up when we find ourselves experiencing different Essential Qualities. For example, the color blue often represents Understanding. Green can indicate Growth or Compassion. Yellow often suggests Curiosity or Joy. Two of my favorite colors are black and red. Red stands for Strength, including the underlying strength of a powerful emotion, like anger. What I love, is that pent-up anger can be experienced, and then released into new creative energy. Black has opened my eyes right from the beginning. Black led me to directly experience Its Power. Maybe this is why working with colors in my collages is so compelling, so satisfying and calming.

◆ ◆ ◆

Now, my husband and I are getting ready to go on another trip. He always waits until the last minute to pack; I like to pack four or five days in advance so I can add and subtract things that make sense for the particular trip. My suitcase is red. It's perched on top of my husband's dresser. In fact, he has to move it a bit every time he goes into his underwear drawer. The following is what occurs in our "red suitcase" husband/wife drama.

I'm in our bedroom putting something in my red suitcase. My husband is off in another room, but we can still hear each other. My husband says something to me from the far room.

Me (M): Wait a minute, I'm packing my suitcase.

Husband (H): What suitcase?

M: The one on top of your dresser.

H: There is no suitcase on my dresser.

M: Yes, there is. It's been there for days. (I'm getting a little upset.)

H: No there isn't.

M: Yes, there is. It's red for God's sake. I'm standing here putting my shorts in it.

H: That can't be. I would know if a suitcase was there; that's where I get my underwear and socks.

M: No response.

> *My world turns flaming red. I am fuming. I am aflame. I am so angry that I cannot speak. OMG, this is over the top. I pause. Wait. I feel the anger. Slowly, my mind empties. After about three minutes, just like that, the anger dissolves.*

I'm amazed. What just happened? And then the information is downloaded; If my husband can't see a red suitcase that's right in front of his eyes, how can he see **me**? Yep, the old imprint of not being seen had reared its ugly head once again. I have more work to do. But this experience shows me that ***there are greater powers working within me. These powers take me beyond my old imprints into a healthier perspective.***

♦ ♦ ♦

I have been experiencing a lot of Essential Black lately. So, I decide to sit down and review the many ways that Black has been shown to me.

When my first husband died, I experienced Black as a scary black hole, into which I could fall, but after a while the Black became a velvety softness.

In Holotropic Breathwork, Black led me to directly experience Its Power. It threw me energetically into Its frequency. I fell into deep, wonderful, rich, glowing, inter-galactic Blackness. I experienced how this magical Blackness contains everything that has ever existed, and everything that *will* ever exist. Realizing this reality has been awe inspiring, magical and mystical to me—taking me way beyond my usual comprehension.

Later, with the help of a Diamond Heart teacher, I discovered that an inner empty hole was easily breached, when I was able to stay with its experience.

Black has continued to amaze me throughout my spiritual journey. Once, while meditating, I witnessed an uncut, irregular, black-faceted spaceship, turning ever so slowly, deep within intergalactic space. I sensed the indescribable Power of Black. In the depths of reality, Black was generating Essential nourishment, Energy, and Agency to the universe. Later I was to learn that Black was one of the "Diamond Vehicles."

Black also showed up as an Absolute dimension, pulsating throughout every thought, feeling, and sensation. I see that, as this Black energy crystallizes into physical form, it becomes All that *is*: you, an amoeba, India, cement, a tree, and me.

From the higher, un-formed, dimensions, Black is experienced as a teeny-tiny Point that extends all the way to

Ground Zero; here there's a sense of Home Base. I now enter into Blackness with confidence.

Black reveals yet another dimension, its stunning quality of super-refined perception. Black has the amazing capacity to fine-tune and discriminate what is Essential. In a nanosecond, Black can cut through all the layers, to reveal the Truth in any situation. Black is one of my favorite colors.

Airport Anger

Many years later, my second husband and I are at the airport. We make this same trip every year to go to our Diamond Heart group retreats. And every year we get lost in the very same airport. Every year, my husband says he *knows* how to find the particular location to meet up with friends. Every year, when we get lost, I begin to experience a bit of inner panic. I become agitated, angry, then despondent and resigned. My husband assures me that, at this point, this year, he really "does" know the way. I secretly vow not to get upset.

OK, so now we are in the airport looking for the same location. I can tell that my husband, yet again, is unsure of the way. I begin to bristle. I'm gearing up. I have all my fire power ready to go. Just as I'm about to blast him, suddenly, poof, all my anger disappears! What happened? Here I am all ready to give him the "works." I wanted to; but now there is absolutely nothing to say. All I can feel is love for my husband. I see that my usual fortress has somehow just blossomed into love.

Again, I realize that things are just happening to me, beyond my usual patterns. I actually have no control; "Being" is just doing Its thing.

Walking in Love

Back home, I continue to have unusual experiences on my daily walks. I believe the three experiences that follow all have something to do with the underlying Love, which lays within each of us human beings, whether we realize it or not.

◆ ◆ ◆

So, I'm walking along the bay, and I hear a strange sound, like metal clanking. Up ahead, I see a woman lying face down on the metal bench. Her purse is abandoned on the ground. She is crying so hard that the bench is shaking and clanging. As I get closer, I can hear her words, "I can't go on, I can't go on. I can't go on." She is in utter despair. I walk over and sit against her side. I don't say a word, don't touch, just sit. Magically my arms hover over her back, close, but not touching. I have no idea of what I'm doing; I'm just doing.

After a while, she turns her head, looks up at me and asks, "Who are you? Are you my guardian angel?"

I say nothing. She puts her head back down. The words, "Just take your time," come out of my mouth.

Her deep sobs continue. After a while she looks up and says, "I can go on now."

"Are you sure?" I ask.

"Yes," she says.

I get up and continue on my walk. I have no idea of what just happened; we never see each other again.

♦ ♦ ♦

I'm walking along, feeling full of love. There's a couple walking ahead of me, holding hands. Up ahead, I see a tall skinny man ranting and raving. He's coming across an irrigation ditch leading up to the sidewalk. Strange.

As the couple approaches him, the man fumes, "Nothing I hate more than a loving @#%# couple."

I'm aware that this could be a difficult situation, but there is no fear. The couple walks closer to the raving man, maybe he's on drugs? Then he spies me, and the couple walks past him. The man is now coming up and out of the trench, just as I reach him. We both stop. Now we are on the sidewalk, face to face.

He says, "I'm @#%# angry!"

"Yes, I can see," I say. We both just stand in place. I have no idea what will happen next.

Then he speaks again, "My name is Harold," he says.

"Nice to see you, Harold," I reply.

We both sort of do a double take, and then walk on having no idea of what just occurred.

♦ ♦ ♦

This morning on my meditative walk, without my usual hat, once again love's abundance is radiating everywhere. I walk past the man cutting the lawn whom I see every day. We always exchange waves. Today, I wave, but he does not.

Twenty minutes later, on my way home, with my head down to avoid the glare of the sun, I hear a faint motor sound way off in the distance. As it gets closer it sounds like a lawnmower, but that can't be because I'm on the edge of a huge asphalt parking lot. Strange. When the sound gets really close, I look up; it's the man I see riding on his mower every day! He has just driven all the way across the huge asphalt parking lot.

He is distraught. "I'm so sorry. I'm so sorry," he says. "I didn't recognize you." He's almost in tears.

"It's OK, it's OK" I say. "I didn't wear my hat today."

"No, no, It's not OK. I didn't see you. I didn't see you," he says, "It's terrible."

He gets off his mower and I comfort him. I can't believe how distraught he is. We hug.

"Are you a spiritual man?" I ask.

"I try to be," he says.

On my way home, it hits me; it's not "me" that he didn't see, it was the Love.

Meeting Hameed for the First Time

I'm at my first worldwide Diamond Heart retreat. This is the first international retreat that I am able to attend. Hameed, himself, will be presenting all week. I'm all excited as I watch as this little man, walking with a crutch, climb up onto the speaker's platform. It's Hameed.

I'm sitting right up front. I am mesmerized as he talks about awareness and how our awareness is usually encumbered and limited by the knowledge we've stored in our minds. He says we need to learn to open our awareness up. We need to take the world in with an **awareness of 360 degrees**. Wow, that has never occurred to me. I decide to practice.

I keep my awareness open to my entire "surround" as I walk around, down the halls, on the way to lunch, and on my afternoon walk. I guess this 360-degree awareness is doing something, because the next morning, I fall in love with a strawberry on my plate!

This morning, Hameed says something during his talk that doesn't make sense to me. When everyone files out for a break, I go up to him to ask for clarification. Since he is still up on the platform, he bends his head way down to reach me, and I lean up to him. Now we are really close, head-to-head. I ask my question; he answers. But it's what happens next that astounds me. When I stand back up to leave the hall, it's like I am floating. I can barely stand up, and I'm crying. I have no idea why.

◆ ◆ ◆

That night I have extensive dreams, which review, and clarify, all the relationships I've had with men in this life. It all plays out before me and makes a great deal of sense. I see that as a child, I loved one man, my father, who betrayed me. I am also shown how very lucky I have been in love, drawing truly loving men to me, like my late husband, my late partner in South Africa and my current husband.

The next morning, as I was describing this amazing experience to one of the Diamond Heart teachers, he said, "Yes, it's like that when you actually get into Hameed's aura."

Unexpected Relationships

A few months later, I'm with my usual Diamond Heart group. This retreat is about relationship. For two days now, we've been meeting in student pairs; each time talking about how we actually experience the truth in the other person. By late afternoon, we've met with numerous individuals. My last interaction for the day turns out to be quite a surprise.

Our meeting starts out innocently enough. My fellow student tells me how he has had such a good day; he has made a number of new friends. I mention that I'm more interested in discovering how we experience each other than I am in making friends. Well, that starts it. This man lays into me with both guns blazing. He tells me that I am "way worse" than his mother; and calls me every name in the book. For the life of me, I cannot muster up any sort of upset. I am completely calm. **Somehow, this is all just happening and it's not in the least offensive**. This just makes my inquiry partner even madder. Finally, he gets up and leaves the room.

I don't know what happened. Still feeling quite neutral, I go to dinner, and then off to bed. I'm not sorry for what occurred today, but I do want to straighten out our relationship. So, I decide I'll ask him to talk in the morning.

The next morning, in the hall, my last inquiry partner from yesterday walks quickly by me and says he'd like to talk to me later. I say, "Good." Instantly, an image of two chairs pops into my head and a man is like sitting on my lap. This seems odd, but I just forget about the image.

After breakfast, the two of us just "happen" to come together as we are entering the classroom. The door "happens" to unexpectedly be propped open by two chairs. And I suddenly ask if the student would sit down next to me and put his legs over my lap.

> *Instantly, it's like he is sitting on my lap. He immediately folds himself into my arms. I spontaneously just rock him like a baby, patting him on the behind and loving him. He cries uncontrollably; both of us just continue to hold each other and rock.*

This entire experience was amazing. I realize that when my soul is relaxed, I find myself in a neutral dimension. Yesterday, I wasn't triggered when attacked; in fact, I couldn't be because my soul understood that nothing really personal was happening. Life was just expressing Itself. Life had come through for me by providing the scenario, images, words and expressions that actually led to love. Yes, **when the soul is "in charge," incredible things happen.**

During this same week-long workshop, one of my friends comes up to me and asks if I would work with her in another room, away from the other students. She found it difficult to touch or be touched. I said, "Sure." She proceeded to walk us into an adjoining room, closed all the blinds and put a chair up against the door to secure it. She explains, "ever since the rape I have not been able to let anybody touch me. But I would like you to work with me on that now."

We sit close together on the floor. She tentatively allows me to touch her gently on the arms and then the legs. As we continue, she allows me to hold her and rock her. Finally, I ask, "Would it be OK for me to put my hand on your chest?"

She says, "We could try." I very gently lay my hand over her heart. She immediately places her hand over mine. This is an exquisitely intimate moment. The next morning, she tells me our experience together had helped her to "expand" her life. And it surely had affected me also. We are both so grateful for how relationships can develop.

Underlying Blueprints

Another day, I had a private session with my teacher. During our interaction, my inner window was in a completely open zone, where anything could happen; but what occurred next was beyond anything I ever could have imagined.

All of a sudden, a large flying saucer-like object comes zooming at me; I actually duck reflexively to avoid it hitting me in the head. This looming mechanism is enormous and somehow threatening. Now, it's hovering further away so I can examine it more clearly. This structure is HUGE, metal-like and overpowering. It's painted in camouflage colors of beige, gray, khaki, and olive. This whole scenario makes absolutely no sense to me; but the camouflaged object affects me deeply.

I puzzle about this experience for much of the day. Later, my window was wide open again, but this time a quite different image appears.

My inner screen fills with rich blackness, which begins to populate strands of diamonds. The strands form into a bird-like cage, beautifully constructed. The diamondized wires are spread far apart, all faceted and sparkly. This structure is stunningly beautiful and freeing; any occupant of such a cage would never be limited or tethered. What a contrast to my earlier vision.

Before going to bed, I get the "hit." I'm flooded with information that comes from above and explains what happened today. The flying saucer object, and bird cage image, are underlying blueprints of Life! They are templates of structures that lay in the deeper realms. The flying saucer object represents the ego structure. Now the camouflage paint makes a whole lot of sense. The ego structure only shows me the surface of who I think I am, all my learned, acquired beliefs; but this is not really who I am. The open bird cage image represents the underlying structure of Essence. The beautiful diamondized bird cage is not really a cage at all; it's a **wide-open structure that represents the underlying Essential Blueprint from which I come. This Essential structure is supportive, organic, and free; it contains all possibilities for humankind on planet Earth**.

Wow, who knew; I could never even have imagined this.

Intense Experiment

Another year has passed. I'm at yet another Diamond Heart retreat. During one of our weekly sessions, the teachers try out a new "experiment," after all, we'd been working together for years. They ask us to experiment with our animal natures. Well, from my perspective, the room goes wild; chaos erupts everywhere. My nervous system catches on fire. I crouch down on the floor and cover my head with my coat. I can see that a teacher has come over and is on his knees by my head. The noise and chaotic activity continue to buzz. I can't stand it. I make myself get up and go out into the hall. I'm shaking like a leaf, incapacitated, crouched in the hall by myself. The teachers are no longer around.

Finally, a friend comes out into the hall to check up on me. I whisper, "Please find a teacher to come; I'm having a very hard time." When the teacher arrives, he tries to calm me down. "You should have a drink of water," he says. I raise my bottle of water up to my mouth, but I'm shaking so badly, that the water goes everywhere but into my mouth. "Well, I guess that isn't going to work," I say. My friend then offers me her water bottle, "Here try mine." Her bottle is different; it has a tiny little spout on it, sort of like mini sippy cup. I put that little spout into my mouth, and instantly, like magic, I am transformed! My entire body relaxes. I'm astounded. I had never been breast-fed, but somehow, I know this is what an infant feels like when drinking from its mother!

For the remainder of that session, I'm shaking like a leaf. I sit way back in the room, away from people, along with two supportive teachers, my friend, and my "bottle." I realize, that during the experiment, I had regressed back into the incubator once again. This shows me how **early imprints are still affecting my present-day nervous system.** Guess, there's still some meat on those "incubator bones" that wants to be released.

Perfect Student

I'm at yet another Diamond Heart retreat, high up in the Colorado mountains. I've been with Diamond Heart for thirteen years now. I've attended scores of workshops and retreats. I'm like the perfect student. I inquire and practice being present every day, with varying success. But somehow, I'm beginning to get glimpses, feelings of being boxed in, like I've developed some sort of Diamond Heart shell or encasement. Strange.

While walking with other students to dinner, I see, in a very subtle way, how I am being bound and limited by familiar Diamond Heart structures, concepts, beliefs, exercises and routines. This has all been quite unconscious. It feels a bit strange, so I put it in the back of my mind and continue to walk to dinner with my friends.

Choiceless Exit

It is very early. My retreat roommate is still sound asleep. I'm all relaxed in bed. My eyes are closed. Suddenly it happens. I have a vision.

> *An immense white lotus blossom appears in my head. It has many petals, each one is lined in brilliant, glowing, white light. The lotus shines out from a deep, rich, black, velvet-like, Blackness. I am astounded. Intrigued. Oops, the lotus disappears. I watch.*

> *My experience becomes more visceral. I'm like a snake shedding its skin. I watch as my old dried-up casing slips away.*

The vision is as simple as that. But instantly I have the feeling that I've *already* left Diamond Heart. It's over. I'm gone. It's not like I made a choice, it just happens. I am dumbfounded.

◆ ◆ ◆

While talking to my teacher at breakfast, I realize that I am speaking about Diamond Heart in the past tense!

"See that," I say, "I just spoke in the past tense."

She responds, "Staying in the school is not everyone's destiny."

"Well, you're staying," I retort.

But I know I'm leaving the school. From that moment on, I never, even for a second, questioned moving on. I told Hameed that I felt like I was on a shining star, leaping joyfully into the unknown. And it felt good.

Life is My Teacher Now

It's been years since I left Diamond Heart, and I'm still doing the "work," as Hameed would say. Being on my own is a pleasure. I don't have to travel any more. I love the tropical weather in which I live. Every morning I meditate. I take meditative walks through the garden. I say "good morning" to birds and trees, individual flowers and butterflies, sometimes a homeless person too. I also walk along the bay in the evening, and out in the hall when it's too rainy or dark.

I continue to do inquiries with a number of my spiritual friends from my Diamond Heart and Thomas Hübl days. We help each other expand through the highs and lows. I'm also blessed to continue experiencing all kinds of new dimensions and frequencies. New expanses continue to occur. I never know what will happen next; it all comes unbidden and I love it.

The more I practice, the more I am able to I keep my "window open." I'm not as reluctant to go deeply into discomfort, because I've learned that **the greater the level of discomfort that I am able to process, the more "old stuff" I am able to release, the more I will be shown of the blissful ground of True Nature that lays underneath**.

◆ ◆ ◆

I jump out of bed and go to the computer.

It's HERE. ALIVE! AWAKE! AWARE!

Centralized intensity

Takes up residence!!

Moves in, takes over all the rooms

Gets the body out of bed

Types words on this machine

Divine, royal, purple and white

Wants to EXPRESS, SHOUT, PROCLAIM

From mountain tops, dungeons, and drones

This is Intelligence, Supreme

It dominates and subsumes all

It shines its dark, radiating, light all over the place

Encompassing everything

Absorbing, destroying, creating itself, and the world all at once

The Eternal Flame, One, True, Ever-present Moment

TOTAL AWAKENESS

It's HERE!!

There is Celebration, Equanimity, and Joy

◆ ◆ ◆

I'm contemplating. There's a stark, aware, wide-open field. Within deep spaciousness, I'm aware of a pulsating membrane. It's alive and conscious. This amazing, delicate "structure" is moving. It is pushing forth everything that can be perceived from the human domain—me, you, essential qualities, the moon, palm trees, and coconuts. I am actually this throbbing Nothingness, this open universal alive awake-ness.

*There's a sense of complete freedom. I witness that **"Is-ness" is just Isssssssing away**. This place says, "yes" to everything, war, famine, joy, baby toes and buildings. All is welcome. No "thing," whether it be a thought, sensation, feeling, quality, or experience is ever turned away. **Everything has the freedom, the potential to be deeply seen and felt**.*

My usual Sunday routines are sliding away. No special breakfast is needed. I'm not desiring my most comfortable "hang around" clothes. I'm really not "doing" anything at all. **Being is just having its way. There is no "me," in fact I am the entire field**. There is no stickiness, no identification. I see how my usual beliefs and habits generate, maintain, and reinforce the usual "Barbara."

But today, everything that comes up within this space, is just allowed and slips away. I bow down.

Pure and Simple Freedom

Meditating, pen in hand: It's quite weird how life works, back and forth, up and down; yet I see that this is a perfect configuration. It's a perfect set up. It's a perfect mechanism for learning, adapting, experiencing, changing, expanding, and evolving into all that a human being is actually designed to be.

I see, **as human "vehicles," we are designed for transformation**. **We are designed for receiving and transmitting**. *My body is shaking, vibrating. I see subatomic particles, platelets, moving, jumping around, actively playing and transmitting through space. It's like looking through a microscope at a slide of living matter.* **I see, feel, and sense pixelated activity.** *I am thankful for this action, this agency. I thank the particles for their contribution, without which my perceived physical body would not be.*

My, my, what a mixed up, tangled meditation this is. I'm aware of how I love the way this pen is writing; it's gliding over the page. It's alive and having a grand old time. Maybe this is how a two-year-old experiences life? What fun. I witness how everything is alive. The "me," and the "I" are just baked into the mix. Yowie! **This is True Freedom—no analysis, no judgment, unadulterated freedom**. *Pure. Simple.*

Chapter 4: Mystical Deepening Days

Today I listened to a mystic on the internet; the words that he spoke could have been the words coming out of my own mouth! I'm delighted. Intrigued. So, I do a little research. Thomas Hübl is a modern-day mystic. He teaches using present-day concepts and language. For example, Thomas teaches that human beings are like "bio-computers." We receive and process information from the dimension of Universal Intelligence. He then goes on and compares our "inner" computer abilities to our outer technological advancements, which are happening in the density of Earth. He talks about receiving "downloads" from higher intelligence.

Wow, this is the same kind of information that's been coming to me. I sign up for a course with Thomas Hübl online. This will be some exciting new stimulation for my spiritual practice.

Thomas Online

I love what this guy is saying. Thomas talks about karma, our cosmic address, collective consciousness, transparent communication, and grounding ourselves in the "marketplace." He talks about things that help explain how, and why, I've been having all these crazy kinds of dimensional experiences for years. Finally—I'm getting a deeper understanding of why, and when, I find myself experiencing different energetic frequencies. Lower frequencies bind me to my usual way of seeing. Lower frequencies make up the actual physical parts of humanity and the Earth. Higher frequencies occur when I go beyond my usual limits of perception. They take me into the more subtle dimensions that transcend time and the material world.

I listen to each session. Then I edit it carefully for my own use. Thomas's native language is German, mine is English. So, as I carefully sort through each sentence, and apply what I know spiritually, these edits considerably expand my consciousness. I'm like a pig in you know what.

Karma

Thomas explains that, when we are born, we come down through layers and layers of previous human experience. We pick up this information and bring it into this lifetime with us. So, in effect, we come into this life loaded with other lifetimes of human knowledge. Most of us are completely unaware that we are carrying around this collected bag of experience from our ancestors, and from humankind in general. It wears me out just thinking about it.

Direct Experience of the Collective

Meditating: A rocky, crunchy, inner crust is breaking apart. There's a sense of grief and a sense of joy at the same time; what a strange combo. It is all so confusing and mixed-up. What's going on here? Something wants to come up, but what?

Later while soaking in the tub, it comes to me, Oh, wow, I think the grief has something to do with the confusion that happens when a person dies a sudden, unexpected, or traumatic death.

A chain of scenarios whips through my head—my father's suicide, my first husband's dying beside me in the car, the murder of a loved one in South Africa, the young man who committed suicide and landed on a ledge beneath my window. I can feel his confusion right now. I think of deaths in Europe and Asia and Africa, all around the world. And now, weirdly, a feeling of joy arises. It's the joy of leaving the physical body! It's the joy of entering the domain of the formless!

On the other hand, I can feel a common reservoir of confusion that gets activated when a person dies a sudden, unexpected, or traumatic death—it's a feeling of being lost, not knowing what happened, or where one is.

I realize that often, unconsciously, I contract when hearing about death. I inwardly recoil and want to avoid any real feelings that may be lurking inside. But here, my direct experience of grief led me into the bandwidth of collective consciousness. I got to actually experience what happens when someone dies unexpectedly. Now I see that it's my responsibility to feel into this confused reservoir when it comes up. Maybe this collective "cosmic address" can help dissolve some of the confused or uncomfortable feelings that occur. I will be paying much closer attention.

Burning Karma Helps the World

It just came to me. **When I dissolve my own feelings, like isolation, separation or abandonment, I am actually burning up karma for all humankind!** My role in this life is to be a little self-absorber! I want to scoop up the sense of the isolated self, to burn up the false-ness of who I am. I want to burn up beliefs that no longer serve me. I want to burn up my fear of limitation and separateness.

I want to open all doors to the truth and the present-day world.

> *Hold on, a window is opening up. It's raining! Big chunks, and little tidbits, of my ego are falling away, being absorbed, melted, washed clean. My ego belief systems, concepts and patterns are being bombarded, blowup, annihilated. Tiny bits of old knowledge are sifting out as they become seen and acknowledged. And now I am shown that there is really no difference between my individual ego mind and the "mind" of all humankind.* **My spiritual "work" is working for the whole world***.*

Living Inside the Tunnel

This morning I'm thinking about all the infinite, boundless, dimensions that I have been able to experience over the years. Just when I'm about ready to give my ego-self a few spiritual brownie points, the higher dimension comes in to set me straight.

Suddenly, I realize how BONDED I am with my personal appearance, my worldly projection, sensation and doing. I'm glued to a familiar "me," this familiar body. This is still unconsciously serving as my net of security. I'm trapped within this internal tunnel of perception.

*Oh, brother, now I'm noticing more. **I have the inclination to go on stage and get involved as a particular person in the day-to-day play that's projecting.** I see that I have also acquired a tunnel of perception in how I view the external world, the marketplace, as Thomas calls it. I have pre-conceived notions about what should be, or probably will occur.*

Now, I'm observing my outside life from backstage. It's like watching a play from behind the curtain. I'm seeing the actors, and how the stage is set up. I'm hearing the script being read. The audience is out front waiting for the performance. This play is like a movie that appears front stage.

*I morph into a different frequency, now the script is just magically emerging. The various dimensions, the inside, outside, you, and me, are differentiated; but I notice that they cannot be separated. **Life energy amalgamates as it comes down into the density of everyday life**.*

Mind/Space/Time: How Things Work

I'm sneaking out of bed at 3am in the morning. Here's my notebook, where's my sweater; I have to write this down.

It's my mind that makes up the world! It's my mind that manifests what I'm thinking, and projects that information— the thoughts, concepts and feelings out into the world. When I'm sleeping, it does the same, but then my usual, learned mind is One, so I can dream, fly and have adventures. Now, I realize this is also what's happening in my waking moments too. I've learned to limit my projection to what I've come to believe is true. This is why, when my usual mind disappears, I easily go into different planes and have adventures.

Oh, and then there is space! My little mind sees in linear, physical terms. I have to go across the room to get to the door. But in this infinite space/place, anything can happen. That's why the other night, when I got up to go to the bathroom, I discovered that my physical body was still in bed. I had to go get it. Yow, an out-of-body experience.

Another download, Time. Time only exists in the physical, linear domain. But in this more open field, when I keep my window open, there's no time what-so-ever. There is only, this, very, present, now, moment. And this moment is eternal. It is the only moment; past and future are merely concepts that I have acquired, only figments of my imagination. I can see how this one, eternal moment is constantly changing, morphing. I realize this is how I am able to experience so many different worlds.

I'm morphing right now. Pen stops writing. I hear my husband in the next room making sleeping noises. I'm becoming empty. This is an entirely different frequency. My body is sort of humming. I'm alive, awake. I see that I am Everything and Everywhere, at the same time. There is no local me. There is no place, space, or dimension in which I do not exist. I hear the sound of Silence in my head. I feel my feet, cold, on the floor, I'm heading back to bed.

◆ ◆ ◆

In the morning, I recall my 3am frenzy. It's not like I haven't experienced the energy of mind, space, and time before; but **when I experience the combined energy of mind, space, and time, I really get activated**. It's this amalgamation of energy that wakes me up at 3am. **It's this active, unbidden agency that brings in deeper realizations and urges me to move on**. I see how my practices, like meditative walking and writing crazy things in my journal, are fueled by this combination of energy.

Sky Consciousness

I've been noticing how my day-to-day experience is changing. Sometimes, as soon I step out my door, my world becomes radiant—colors vivid, blades of grass distinct, wind magical, swirling around me. At other times, when I'm walking outside, my entire "surround" is so magnificently beautiful that I find myself crying tears of joy. But this morning I really got a surprise.

I'm sitting in a waiting room, waiting to get my eyes examined. All of a sudden, a bolt of inner lightning hits, almost throwing me off the chair:

*A deep, ever-present, pure, awareness is here revealing that **all states of waking, sleeping, dreaming, dying, and even after life are the same**. They are all composed of this same Sky-Like Consciousness.*

This Sky Consciousness allows everything. It is completely open. Nothing phases it—rain, clouds, thunder, tornados, fire, floods. Everything is allowed to come into the open window of the heart.

*This isn't the way my usual head works; things get stuck and conflicted. But from this sky perspective, I see how Life is constantly birthing and destroying Itself, becoming Itself and moving on. I can feel Life's vibration in the center of my throat and chest; It's radiating, pulsing, and teeming with Its, my, morphing existence. **My consciousness has become sky-like**.*

Magic Carpet Ride

I sense something unknown, unidentified, is coming through. For days I watch and listen in silence. Sometimes it feels like an alien place, very different; there is no sense of belonging, and no need to identify or dock. Sometimes there is just blissful non-attachment. All of this happens at the whim of what's appearing in my inner world, of what's being digested by my energetic system.

I am shown there *is* an inner bio-computer that is displaying ancient knowledge, things that I've learned in this life, and other lifetimes. There's a sense of constant "emergent knowing." Everything in the universe is animating, emerging, and integrating. I suspect what's "breaking through" has something to do with "planetary awareness." This inner sense persists, along with a wild image.

Deep, rich, blackness displays a flying bubble structure, a thick rectangular sheet of unified bubble-knobs. Each bubble-knob displays red, green, and yellow. All knobs are bound together in connective rows. I notice that this flying bubble vehicle is flexible; it's a floating, alive, organism. And it is gliding through endless planetary space. I am intrigued. Whoa, now I realize that I am in all the bubbles. I am in all locations at the same time. But somehow, I am also riding, housed, in a specific bubble. I am located in the far-left-hand corner.

*Instantly, I find myself riding within the flying bubble vehicle with a surround of operational mechanisms. This is like the chamber of Life's Encoded Information! And this body of unfolding wisdom is learning about Itself! Life is learning more about how to download spiritual light and energy into a terrestrial human body. I had things up-side down. **I am, we, Are Life Force, True Nature, Divinity that is learning to become embodied.** We, as receptive bio-computers, are learning how to most effectively create an advanced human consciousness, one that is embodied on planet Earth. This flying bubble sheet is like the Mother Board of Life! I don't yet understand this, but I get the sense that there is a Code of Life.*

Zoom, I am shown there is always an earlier choice point for human actions, in both the horizontal and vertical dimensions. There is always a way to balance divinity and a mature ego.

This is way above my current knowledge and ability. I will need to observe, practice, and learn how to choose Life before being pulled into my usual thinking realm. I will have to learn more about the flying-bubble machine and my relation to it.

A number of days pass, as this flying-bubble-sheet-vehicle shows more of Itself to me. Now I realize I am actually riding in this flying-bubble-vehicle. And I somehow understand there is an underlying, central Command Center of Power, Influence and Authority that is slowly moving towards more and more Order. This is truly wild.

Transparent Communication

Today, I met with one of my inquiry friends. We've been meeting for several years; we've developed a deep friendship and spiritual relationship. The two of us often openly discuss what's going on in our inner lives. It seems like our consciousness is becoming more and more agile, combined realizations come faster and more often.

Me (M): Hey, are you still feeing terrified when you wake up in the morning?

Friend (F): Actually no. I just realized that I haven't felt like that ever since I moved. But now that you mention it, I can see that it's actually here also. It's like there is a bigger field that's open right now and there is this smaller field that holds this terror.

M: Let's just stay and see what happens. I'm getting a sense of your early childhood.

F: Yes, I really had to pay close attention to my mother. She could be so hurtful. I always was expected to play out whatever version of myself that she wanted of me. I had to do this to survive.

M: I'm getting the sense of being alone and frightened and helpless.

F: Wow, there was just a shift when you said that. I think that what you are saying now has more to do with your own childhood than it does about mine.

M: You may be right. I don't really know. I see you as being very attuned to another's perspective. And now something seems to be coming in even more; I get the sense that right now you are coming from the bigger field. I see how you had to learn to really be tuned-in from early on and how this skill of attunement has helped you in your work.

F: Barb, you just gave me a gift. I never saw it like this. Do you really think I am so "attuned" as you call it?

M: Definitely. I see the difference even when you are with me. You are so skillful in pointing out when I am experiencing something that is not really where you are coming from. It really helps me to recognize a distinction in my experience. I can count on you to tell me. So maybe I am just experiencing my own childhood.

F: When you say that there is another shift. I see that you are just expressing what is actually in the field right now! It's not you and it's not me. It's just here.

M: Yikes! I can see that this is just materializing in the field! I have to tell you what happened at the gym the other day. I was on one of the weight machines and it hit me like a thunderbolt, "My bones are everybody's bones!" It may not sound like much, but it opened up a whole new realm—beyond Oneness and Unity.

I understand there is only one Energy, one Beingness, one Nothingness. There is only one soul, one realm of emotion, thought, ego, blood, tree, and everything. This One dynamic energy is displaying, manifesting, transforming with Itself, as Itself. I'm astounded, amazed, in awe. This makes so much sense—how a person can feel into, and experience another's bones, and with intent, the pixels redistribute themselves, heal, and transform.

F: It seems like we are tapping into something universal that comes with the field of childhood. And it's what is in this field at this very moment. We are part of IT. It's just the field of this moment. It's not you or me; it's the human, experiencing, part of the One reality!

M: Yes, and it is a Singularity—a solid block of Reality too. It's magically morphing, displaying and transforming Itself. I am, we are, this Nothingness cloaked with this human realm of experience. And somehow there is a responsibility to be present to the presentation, to abide, and commit to a conscious awareness.

F: This is so cool. Let's schedule another inquiry date.

Hearing the Whisper

I need to go v-e-r-y slowly. I want to hear what is going on inside my inner world. I want to tune into the sound of silence that I'm hearing. I am beginning to understand this is a matter of frequency, like tuning into different stations on a radio. Hard Rock music is different than Classical. I have the sense that the frequency of anger is quite different than the frequency of the divine.

I watch. When lower frequencies come in, like anger, or shame, or disgust, I somehow get thrown off kilter. I'm no longer plugged into my source. I'm more foggy, unaware and bogged down. When higher downloads come, they are clearer, purer. My perception is more expansive, colors are more vivid, life is easier. When this happens, I experience how *everything* is energy. I experience how higher energy-frequencies operate in a much more effective way in my daily life; they buoy me up.

So, I want to develop my inner whisper and my sense of stillness. I want to learn how to stay present, even though my mind wanders off every few moments. This seems critically important because I want to hear the whisper and keep my window open. I want to clear out any old energy that builds up during the day. I want to have enough inner space to be me, to be authentic.

Now, I'm walking in the hall. Wait a minute, something's coming in. It wants to be seen and heard. Let's see. Oh, this is not the little ego me. It's the big me! It's the Essential Me. The Essential Me is insistent, it is pushing forth forcefully, showing Itself! It wants to be seen and heard in the physical world.

I wonder what the Essential Me would say if it could talk. I ask. I listen as Essential Me talks:

> *"I am Reality. I am here for you to bring me forth into the world. This is a necessity, a responsibility. (I quickly feel inadequate and small.) But you are not. You understand what I am saying, what I want. It's time to put your childish habits aside. I, Reality, am being restricted, restrained and contained within your cosmic address. I need you to help me come through you, through your cosmic address, through your humanness out into the world. The view from here is expansive and essential. You need to be a part of the dynamic unfolding that is happening to the human race.*

"Reality does not discriminate or judge. Judgments and comparisons cease to exist. These things merely register, and equalize, but they don't become activated. Karma, history, habit, toe cramps, and tight hips are all lovingly, and evenly, held. They are equally included as they arise naturally, organically, in your consciousness. You just watch. Listen. You will see them come up and then you will see them disappear into the huge vastness that I am."

Wow, that was unexpected. I pause. ***I realize there is a wisdom body available. We humans are actually evolutionary whisperers.*** These are the words that come to me now, and I know they speak the Truth.

Grounding

The richness of my body is just beginning to blossom, dropping deeper, subtler, physical petals into my day-to-day life. I still tend to stay in my head, rather than come down into my body. I'm going to meditate and watch.

> *Now, I can feel my energy going down and down and down—threading itself, twisting, and turning, screwing itself deeply into the Earth. **Oh yeah, here is support, true support!** This sturdy support also **brings a sense of stature and regal-ness. Then reverence —** a profound, alive, sense of respect floods in. I bow down.*

I realize that ***active awareness, and physical participation, are required to learn how to become more***

grounded. I want to become more aware of my body on an everyday basis. I need to pay more attention when I am walking, exercising, or at the gym, not just when I meditate. I think I'm usually doing physical things quite absent mindedly.

I pray that I may choose to abide in my body each moment as I go through my day. I know that there is much more to learn about my physicality.

Embodied Awareness

I haven't been able to walk comfortably ever since my first husband died many years ago. Today It's worse. I feel like an old man who can barely walk. My body feels slow, burdened. My foot is clutching inside my shoe, yet again. I settle into this sluggish, limping gait, then realize there are layers and layers of karma wanting to come through. I relax, accept, and embrace this karmic package.

> *Suddenly hundreds of pieces of accumulated information are flooding in. My toes clamp down. I get the sense that I am literally hanging onto the incarnate world by my toes, unwilling to give up the old images and identifications that have made up my life's story.*
>
> *But my inner world is still morphing. I can see that this old story is NOT who I am. I am changeless, yet at the same time, ever-moving and transforming. Now I'm like a butterfly being pushed out beyond some cocoon-like structure. I'm becoming, metabolizing, moving through the incarnate world like the wind. Wow, now*

my body feels huge, solid, substantial. Everything is transparent. Tidbits of love and joy are raining down.

◆ ◆ ◆

Today, while exercising at the gym, I find myself wearing a robe of silver and gold. **The gym is being people-ed**, Mike doing sit-ups, Susan rowing, Norm lifting weights. The gym is being "populated" and "thing-ed" with TV's, music, and exercise machines. Light is shining through everything— cars outside the window, people exercising inside, bikes and brains, including my fingers and bones. **The physical, incarnate world is transparent! Yet I am firmly rooted right here on Earth**, feet on pedals.

Driving home, I realize that I've given up trying to figure things out. I know that what just happened at the gym is beyond my brain's capacity to understand. Forget the analysis. Forget the interpretation. Just keep my inner window open. Allow whatever comes and move on. These are dimensional fluctuations of the Living Energy. As an aspect of the billowing, undulating, Energy doing Its thing, I am learning to ride the waves that swell above my usual rational perspective.

Realizing the Dream While Awake

This morning, I'm lying-in bed, and poof!

Realize I am this ALIVE AWAKENESS. I AM AWAKE WITHIN THIS DREAM. I watch as this vast, alive, awake-ness looks out, seeing Itself shining through, and emanating throughout my physical, daytime, *dream. Wow, **this is what is actually happening all the time, but I am usually unaware**.*

*From this space/place, it is evident that all manifestation, **everything that arises, from the Silent Nothingness to the usual "me" perspective, is actually a WIDE-AWAKE DREAM!** Now, I'm observing my Self waking up to this dream, being awake within this dream, and operating as the Dream Itself.*

I see how the dream forms my surround, the way that I see day to day. I am usually clothing myself with the familiar— walls of the bedroom, ceiling, feelings, things. I clothe myself in concepts, thoughts and beliefs. I become a subject, separate from other, from object. I begin to judge, compare, and identify myself through images, habits, and personality. I begin to manipulate my experience. I become conditional.

*Heavier consequences occur. I morph into self-blame. I withdraw, contract, and become re-active. I puff up or close down my experience. **When I am not awake**, I take on more and more layers through my senses, thoughts, society, and karma. **I add layers of heaviness; these layers materialize and BECOME the dream in which I live**.*

*But, **when I am awake, within the Dream**, I no longer need instructions, I no longer act from a hidden blueprint; **I simply BECOME the dream**.*

Making breakfast, this alive Awake-ness takes a blue dish from the cabinet, moves the spatula, and feeds Itself fried eggs. Pure magic, simple, sensational, fascinating. Free.

Energy Trapped Between Death and Life

During my regular morning meditation, my body begins jerking violently; whoa, here we go again. Something huge, and frozen, is waking up!

*It's mammoth and unknown. It's alive and powerful. It fills all perceptions, layers, and dimensions. I notice an inner membrane is confining my perception, like an inner sausage stuffed full of bits and pieces of meat, grime and grizzle. **There is cellular memory here, from the collective, and from all my learned thoughts, feelings and behaviors in this lifetime**. I feel a bit nauseous. But wait; there is still an open awareness.*

*I realize that I am finding, feeling into, and receiving information. **I am allowing, following, and watching parts of Life releasing Itself through my bodily jerks**. On closer inspection, I see that I am wrapped in a membrane-like structure where energy is trapped, can't escape. It feels tight. Nebulous. I wait.*

The download comes. Wow, I somehow know that this is energy that was trapped at the time of physical death; it's energy that was not able to release itself before coming into the next life.

Now one end of the membrane-structure dissolves. My nervous system relaxes. I see the solidified part; it's hard and calcified. Knock, knock, it's harder than rock. At the same time, I notice a strong, endless, column of light extending up through the center of my body. Energy is pumping in love and relaxation! The pressure is dissipating. I sit more deeply in my chair. There's a slight sense of joy and release from bondage.

I can still feel the stiffness of the structure, of being frozen, unable to move. So, I feel into the stiffness. Now there's an awareness of killings, of people drowning, and flashes of war; more souls are being caught and bounded in this in-between realm of life and death. There is a mournful sense of sorrow, then grief. **Wait, old desires and fears are now being overshadowed by the divine. I realize I'm Home! The ultimate support is never <u>not</u> here.**

Ancient Wisdom Brings Knowledge and Joy

What is happening? Something is moving fast. There is light, and then a troubling darkness. I'm writing as fast as I can. I am alone. I am constricted.

All of a sudden, I see images of children in places like Syria, Jordan, and Sudan. There's hunger and despair, fear. No hope. **It feels like this helplessness is cellularly embedded in me; it's as if I am these troubled children!**

The light returns and begins dissolving this energetic address of the children and me. I'm morphing again, now there's a very tight rubber band encircling my lower diaphragm. There is absolutely no movement here. Life is cut off. There is no access. I am squeezed into a very tight spot.

Oh brother, thoughts of death and destruction arise. I witness images of predatory animals, the hacking of bodies, machetes, swords, explosions. This is terrible. **Another download of information occurs; I realize that this is the same cosmic address, the same frequency of consciousness as 9/11 and ISIS.**

From this realm, there is no-where to move, no-where to go, no alternative; inner life is completely cut off. The outer world is filled with abject hate and despair. **This consciousness frequency is compelled to hate, kill, and act destructively upon the outer world. No alternative is seen. It is kill or be killed.**

It takes a long while for the light to move this depressed energy through my body—but gradually, very gradually, the light sifts through and gently falls down into my base. But now, my base feels very different. It is tremendous, palatial, much greater than usual. It occurs to me that this base is actually the container for the entire world; it's the projection of Life Itself!

This Light holds all of humankind. There's a sense of ancient wisdom, communication, connection here. There's a wealth of human knowledge stored within this common, elevated, LIVING space.

I continue to contemplate. I was just thrown into the actual frequency of 9/11. I was experiencing the actual cosmic address of this occurrence. I see now, how vividly these kinds of occurrences have been recorded in a certain bandwidth of energy.

When I let go of my usual perceptual limitations, I open to infinite possibility; here I am shown the specific seed point, or original cosmic address, of occurrences that have happened throughout human history. This seems huge.

But in retrospect, I realize, at other times, I have been shown that **each human being has his or her own cosmic address, an indelible place of divine origin**. We are all part of this ever-changing magical, living medium.

Thomas in Person

I'm now on an in-person retreat with Thomas. I want to check him out, see who he really is. My head just comes up to his chest, didn't realize he was so tall when I saw him online. I also find him to a kind, sensitive, human being and an incredibly effective teacher.

I watch as he literally senses where each student is as they ask a question or present a problem. It is fascinating to watch him work.

Walking Above the Ground

It's the third day at the retreat, I feel like I am walking three feet above the ground. I mention this to Thomas, as he is walking out for a class break.

"Thomas, I feel like I'm floating above the ground. I was placed in a metal incubator with a lid and no windows when I was born." (I'm not quite sure why I say this, but this is all I say.)

When class starts after the break, I feel a hand on my shoulder.

"Thomas asked me to work with you," a teacher says.

"Oh, good, I'll look for you after class," I reply. I am quite surprised to be offered this help.

The teacher continues, "No, come with me now," as she leads me back to a little room. She puts two chairs together, seat-to-seat, facing each other, and asks me to sit. We sit very close.

She puts my knees inside her knees, so I'm all enclosed and feel secure.

> Now, it's like I warp speed back into the incubation again, but this time with adult support. She lets me gently touch her nose, caress her face and touch her hair. I look into her eyes.

> She whispers, "I am here for you. You are wanted in this physical world. You belong."

I sob deeply. Here is acceptance, relief. And I no longer find myself walking mid-air.

Tribal Dance

Later that day, we form into small groups; each person is asked to lead the group in their own personal dance. My dance becomes very basic, guttural. I'm down on the floor on all fours. We all end up crawling around, making weird noises, and having a jolly old time. We become a tribe—united and free. This is my first experience of feeling connected to a tribe!

Standing Up for My Truth

Today was quite the day. It's the last day of Thomas's retreat. Days ago, he gave us a task: Design your personal t-shirt. Write the one phrase that you would most like people to know about you, the one phrase you would never say out loud. Well, my one phrase completely surprises me.

The phrase is I DO KNOW. I realize, in workshops, and with family and friends, I've always underplayed what I actually experience in the spiritual realm. In the past, my parents would ridicule me, and students would give me the "she's weird" look. So, I just never spoke out loud about the profound knowledge that was coming through.

But now it's time to speak out; I'm at a mystical workshop for God's sake. So, I decide I'm going to tell my truth. I'm nervous and afraid, but I am going to do it.

Well, I've been trying to speak out my t-shirt words for three days now, but Thomas doesn't call on me. He will call on anyone but me; the person in front of me, the person in back of me, the person to my side, but not me. I raise my hand very high, again and again. I raise my leg, nothing. It becomes a joke that everyone is in on.

Anyway, today is the last day of the workshop. I'm dying to speak out. Once again, Thomas calls on everyone but me. Finally, as he is closing the workshop, he looks at me and says, "Do you still want to say something?" I look around to see who he is speaking to; I point my finger at my chest, "me?" He nods "Yes."

I am so caught off guard, I just stand up and start talking. I'm confessing to the whole group. I look around, startled, everyone is really here for me! Thomas tells me, "You don't have to work on what's above," as he waves his arms over his head; "You need to come down to the ground with what you know. When you develop your base more, and bring your realizations down, the Earth will become your field, and your mouth will start to open. It is OK for you to speak out."

After class, a number of students come over to support me. But now it's time to leave the workshop. I fly home and experiment with my new mouth.

◆ ◆ ◆

Telling My Truth

I guess I have a deep need to come out because, when I got home, I find myself writing to my sangha, my online spiritual group. This group is comprised of hundreds of people, never mind the 120 that I just confessed to in person.

Dear Sangha members: I am crying as I type my post. I'm afraid I need to tell a bit of history first. I started to wake up twenty years ago when my husband died suddenly by my side. It was like going through life at eighty miles per hour and then hitting a brick wall. Back then I was, at best, an agnostic and when mystical experiences started to come unbidden, I panicked. My "crazy aunt" had been placed in a mental institution because she had "seen God." My family stifled any comments of a spiritual nature. I learned to keep my mouth shut.

Well, I just got back from a week-long retreat with Thomas. I confessed that I've actually had the good fortune to have been shown a great deal of what lays beneath ordinary reality. Thomas told me to come down to Earth and that my mouth would start to open. And now I find myself writing to you. I have never done anything like this before. At the moment I feel humiliated. Past conditioning is having its way. This web site is not for personal coming out. And yet I'm typing this!

Good God, I don't know what will happen now! There is smallness, fear, and sadness present. But it feels like I HAVE to speak out. I have to break out of this self-imposed spiritual cage. Is this online post my trial balloon? Words keep flowing through these typing fingers. I'm all shaky inside. This seems so risky. But you all are a part of this, my, larger spiritual field. I'll stop now. Thanks so much for listening.

Triad Partners Help Clear Old Trauma

I'm on Zoom with my triad partners, who I had met at Thomas's retreat. I start to mention a traumatic incident I had in a past life.

All of a sudden, I find myself in deep dread. Why? I don't understand. I tell my partners, "I don't even know where I am. I'm completely lost." A past life incident comes to mind, the one where I am chained into a wooden cart. I hear big wooden wheels and loud voices. (I thought I had already processed this experience many times; but I was wrong.)

My triad partners are saying, "We're here. We're here." And I am so glad. My central nervous system is aflame, chaotic. My entire body is shaking. A few times I get propelled right up off the chair, covering my face with my hands.

"Barb, you don't have to feel this all at once."

But I am already in some other dimension, "I am in no-man's land. Limbo. There is no quality or emotion. There is no oxygen, no movement. I'm stuck in midair."

And then it hits me: This is actually the same energy that's been trapped for centuries between a physical life that was ending, and another life that had not yet begun. This is astounding!

Wait a minute, this is all occurring at a specific cosmic address! Am I still alive? What am I feeling? Oh God, now my right arm is going to be pulled off. Wait, I realize that I am actually watching the whole occurrence again, this time calmly from up above.

Suddenly, freed from my usual mental perspective, I find that I am viewing from within the past trauma; yet it is happening right now. I can see that I am the entire occurrence, the entire surround. I am the attacker, I am the one being attacked, and I am the attacking itself!

I am witnessing infinite space and physical death. One part is silent and accepting. The other part is in shock, drifting, trapped in a kind of in-BE-tween-ness. All is very detailed and precise. I stop.

My triad partners are still with me, in silence. I can feel their presence.

I say to myself, "Just allow; let the energy do its thing." A sense of Source Energy bursts forth, majestic, powerful, towering up through the sky. Stable. Silent. Brilliance itself is shining forth an unfathomable Knowingness. This higher Brilliance allows and supports everything to just Be as it is.

"Wow guys, now there's pleasure, bliss, and a sublime surrender. I wish I could describe this to you. There's luxurious relaxation. A sense of utter security. I'm sensing generations of support. Ancestors, friends, family, the sangha, saints, avatars are all present."

I realize they are actually always present and available. My entire system is a transparent field, open to the future and to unknown possibility.

I tell my triad partners, "There is deep, deep, gratitude here. **Indescribable love and support are coming out of the blue—freely given.** *It is surrounding our triad."*

My partners concur, "We feel it too."

As our Zoom call ends, I realize that I'm finally gaining Basic Trust for Life Itself, for myself, and for others. ***This journey***

takes place within, and beyond, me, my friends, and all humankind. In this moment there is only peace. The trapped energy has gone.

Seesawing

Meditating: I notice how I often swing, or seesaw, from one dimension to another. One moment, a thought arises, and I career into my old, familiar way of looking at the world. I'm caught. Over and over again I find my mind falling into its well-worn neural network. On the other hand, I know how my energy can shift. Wait a minute, it's doing so right now.

> *I'm no longer in the groove; now there's a wide-open vista! I've swung from my old, familiar, ego-driven perspective to a new feeling of wow-ee. This is actually fascinating. One moment old, another moment new.*

I'm going to try this again. Who am I, the "Barbara" with all her usual patterns, or a "Being-ness" who freely follows what's arising? Seems I don't have a choice, or then again maybe I do. Oh, screw this, I'm not going to think about it anymore.

> *Whoosh, now I'm a streak of bright light, and I'm wrapped around my own cosmic spit! My skewer of light runs up my trunk, right through my head. Wow, I'm like an open network, a radiant energy—arcing through eternity, having multi-level experiences in multi-dimensions, frequencies and universes.*

This is sooo different from the usual groove. Though, I'm thinking, there has to be a more blended, integrated, way of going through life.

Existence/Non-Existence

Today, it's raining so I'm walking in the hall. Suddenly I realize:

> Hey, **Nothing-ness is walking—aware, awake!** There is a huge-ness here, gigantic, monumental. There is power, strength and stay-put-ness. A tiny point appears. My inner screen is now blinking void, point, void, point, void, point. What's going on? There is non-existence and existence blinking together! Take your pick!

I remember, this is what I experienced after Peter's murder—the birthing and destruction of All that is.

The Same Oneness

Lately there's been the sensation that I am being pushed into a new, unknown realm. For days, light has been sending images and messages, old bones that habit digs up.

> I experience teeny tiny ancient bones dangling beneath my pelvis in black spaciousness. A thunderbolt of recognition comes to me: **My heart, my lungs, my bones are the Same as every person's**. I am astonished. Blown away. Yet, I can see this is actually true! We are all part of the Same Oneness. I Know this, but don't quite understand.

> The pieces start to fall into place. I am a central channel of Emptiness—complete Nothingness—Alive and Awake. I am clothed by the world—surrounded by

holographic realms of people, emotions, sensations, and things. I am Brilliance, Beauty, and Magnificence. **I am this Magical Medium**—*changing, creating, displaying, attuned in every way. I am the very Current of Life.* **I am Energy Becoming manifest as water, sky, bridges, boats, eyes, ears, coconuts, boats, rain, emotions, thoughts and dreams.** *I AM ALL.*

Spiritual Friends

At this point in my journey, after many years, I have deep friends with whom to share my inner experiences. I have two triads, which meet to inquire every few weeks, friends from Germany, Scotland, Minnesota, and Canada. Finally, I feel I have love and spiritual support. As I am typing this, there is Emptiness—beautiful and free. I'm like a new-born, but this time the Universal Emptiness is welcoming and warm. I give great thanks.

◆ ◆ ◆

Beyond Light Meditation

Beyond the words there is no light

There is no "I" to connect

Words don't make sense here

No levels or layers appear, just adrift in divine bliss

This-is-ness

When thinking appears, it's as peripheral "rind"

This is Life in the raw

Waking Up

Energy vibrates, pulsates through the physicality of organs, limbs, hormones, blood system

Knowledge of saints and sages is here

Deep space-less-ness, no space, yet fully breathing

Waving energy throughout—like the feel of waters' flow, all awash, swaying, alive, receptive, awake

The entire environment breathes

No desire, no next, no wants, no need to "come down" into a solidified layer of consciousness to have needs, words, wants

Prayer—just allow This-Is-Ness to amalgamate, infiltrate Integrate throughout all levels of existence

At-one-ness, here-ness, at home-ness—all here, present and available—free to partake.

Chapter 5: Days of Deep Release

Today, out of the blue, a good friend sends me an email about a Kundalini yoga class that's starting online. She says if I take this class, "it will change your life." By this time, I understand how the next phase of my personal journey often just pops up quite unexpectedly. So, I sign up with Jai Dev's Foundation Kundalini Yoga Class.

The Journey Begins

There is something about Kundalini yoga that I really like. I'd given up other kinds of yoga long ago. But now, I'm walking and chanting the "Morning Call" every morning. I'm doing at least an hour's worth of Kundalini practices every day. My husband calls this going into my cave. Little does he know what happens when I'm in my private cave. I find that my body shakes and twitches and jerks. I cry buckets of tears, sometimes in joy and sometimes in sorrow. I literally go through boxes of tissue. Something unconscious is releasing, and it feels great. Something wonderful is emerging, and it feels great. Turns out this Kundalini stuff gives me daily support, and huge amounts of physical, psychological, and emotional release.

On my birthday, I tell my husband I'd like to go on a four-day silent retreat. I never have; he has. He helps me find a retreat place. The retreat center tells me that there is no silent retreat at the moment, but I can just come and do my own thing.

Wow, this is fast. I leave on Monday and today is Friday.

I start to think, I've only taken one on-line Kundalini course; I don't even know if I'm doing the poses correctly. I Google Kundalini teachers in my area. I find a master teacher, who has been teaching since 1969. He ought to know what he's doing. I call him up and explain my situation. I'm going on a silent retreat with no instruction. I don't want to have a lesson, but would he just talk with me and give me some advice? "Sure," he says, "Can you come over next Thursday?" "Oh, no," now I'm upset, "I'm leaving on Monday." He says, "Why don't you come to my house on Sunday?"

I do. This man is one of the most kind and compassionate people I've met. He listens. He answers my questions. He instructs. As I leave, he gives me one of his books to borrow, *I Am A Woman: Creative, Sacred & Invisible.*

My Silent Retreat

I set out on my journey. Turns out this retreat place is in the middle of nowhere in a National Park. There is no cell reception. I have to stop every so often to have people tell me where I am. I travel, for what seems forever on this l-o-n-g lonely road. The little white crosses placed on the side of the road give me no comfort. What if I get stuck out here? Finally, I find the retreat center and get settled in a cabin right on the lake, with a long dock sticking out in front.

I am silent. I eat and walk by myself. I chant, reflect, and do Kundalini exercises from morning until when I go to my little puny bed at night. I only leave the compound once.

I drive to a public entrance to the national park. I head down the one-way road and park by a trail. Turns out my foot can't take the bumpy trails, so I try to head back out. But I can't find my way out. And I have the map right in front of me. I try a few times. Then I start to panic. I head down the road, going in the wrong direction, until I find a compassionate soul at a campsite who helps. I explain that I'm dyslexic. (But really, I didn't know it was this bad.)

Finally, back in my cabin, I realize that my panic reaction was way over the top. I go to the Kundalini book, there is this exercise, "Kriya to Relax & Release Fear." I do this for seventy minutes; I release my fear. I reflect on this "panic incident" for the rest of the day. I realize that I've also had an anger pattern, or reaction, for most of my life. I go back to the book and find, "Relieving Inner Anger." I do this exercise for thirty minutes.

Taking a break, I walk out on the dock and watch an osprey dive into the water and retrieve a fish right before my eyes. I go back to my cabin. For good measure, I refer to the book and do "Clearing the Emotions of the Past," fifteen minutes, and its supper time.

That night, I sit on my bed, and put Anger on the bed across from mine.

I ask, "Anger, why have you been with me all my life?"

Anger replies, "To keep you from feeling your broken heart."

I'm stunned. I go back to the book, "Meditation to Heal a Broken Heart." I do this for many minutes and then go to bed. It's been a long day.

◆ ◆ ◆

Now I'm back home, no more solitary retreat, but I continue to do the various Kundalini exercises. Tons of unconscious stuff keeps coming up. My body shakes and jerks, my head moves crazily from side to side, and I cry like a fool again and again. Something even deeper is discharging. I have no idea of what it is. I think this is a good time for me to learn more, so I'm going to dive in and sign up for the more advanced "Dharmic Warrior" course. I'll see what happens.

Dharmic Warrior

Wow, things are really buzzing. I just finished chanting the "White Hole Mantra," one of the chants I learned. I'm at my computer now, typing as fast as I can.

I find myself within a divine, icy, dome, a cathedral. It's like a crystal palace. A divine beauty is flowing through; the bliss is so great, it's almost unbearable. Deep tears. I become aware that this dimension is where the avatars and saints are found. They are silently broadcasting their ancient wisdom and overwhelming love.

This energy comes down into my body, engaging my entire nervous system. My abdomen is aglow with red. It's alive, like molten lava. Surprisingly, there is also a deep sense of healing, and an almost unbearable sense of relaxation, comfort, and support. It is a challenge to actually receive so much. I realize, as humans, we are actually given the entire universe in which to live!

There is Abundance—air, earth, water, plants, love, everything that's needed for us to live and prosper. All is provided.

Wiped Out Yet Something Continues to Function

Walking along the bay, the sun is shining, the birds are singing, and the fish are jumping out of the water, I don't know why.

*OMG! **I don't exist! Just like that, BAM, I'm gone. Wiped out. Erased.** No more "I." Nothing actually exists, including "me." It's incredible, indescribable. I am astonished, wandering, confused. What is happening?*

*This **non-me continues to function**, eating breakfast, driving to the gym. The exercise bike is functioning; there are luminous outlines around all the machines, wires, people and objects, but there is no "me." From this frequency it is impossible to experience anything as good or bad, right or wrong. It just is. There's only Awareness. All day long there is something that continues to see, feel and act, but there is no me.*

This is not the first time I've experienced direct functioning, where the usual "me" is not doing anything or the first time I've experienced direct awareness, but the thing is, each time this happens, it is astounding. Each experience is different. Each experience is always creative, incredible, breath-taking, unique.

All-Together-Ness

The next day, I notice when thoughts or judgments pass through my awareness, they seem like old remnants. I see *when the usual frequency of "me" occurs, I experience a sense of separation.* There is a bit of space between the concept of me and True Nature. But when the usual me fades into the background the magical All-together-Ness comes to the forefront.

> Now, I am like a video camera that's awake and alive. The underlying no-thing-ness prevails. Absolutely sublime. Everything appears as non-personal. *There is no identity, no judgment. I, It, just registers and records the morphing moments. At the same time, a complete and powerful embodiment of functioning is taking place. I become the amalgamation of the moment.*
>
> *I am alive, functioning, moving through time and space as the actual platelets of Being. I am a Living Awareness, a magical morphing, neither existing nor not-existing. What a blessing it is to see this.*

A few months after this experience, because my Kundalini experience is so rich, I decide to go to a week-long retreat with actual Kundalini yogis. I know, I'm only a beginner and not a yogi; but I'm going to do it anyway. It takes a plane ride, three weird bus transfers, and a pick-up by van, to get to the retreat center high up in the mountains.

In Retreat with Real Yogis

Well, I'm here at the retreat, but it turns out I have a problem. I have a weak foot and have trouble walking. I don't usually think much about this condition, but now my problem foot gets in the way. I'm placed in a room where it takes 109 deep steps each way (I counted) to get to the eating and workshop session buildings. Plus, it's about a quarter mile to walk to each session (morning, noon and might).

The first night I set out for the meeting hall. It's cold, dark and rainy. The road is lumpy, semi-paved, and straight up hill. My foot gives out. I see headlights coming on the isolated road, so I put out my thumb, and get picked up. It turns out that it's the teacher and his team. Saved.

Walking back to my room almost does me in. Next day, I ask the person at the front desk if the retreat center could give me a few rides during the week. I also ask a number of students, who have cars; the answers were always no, no, no, no. I am bereft. I'm doomed.

Manifestation Experienced

That night I sleep fitfully. I wake up in the middle of the night. I'm all upset. I've come all this way for nothing. I'm going to have to miss most of the sessions. I notice my roommate, whom I've never met, has arrived during the night and is fast asleep in the other bed. My ego works itself into a frenzy. This is awful.

The next morning, I tell my roommate about the pickle I'm in. I won't be able to attend many of the classes. She says, "I have a car and I want to walk. Use my car all week. I'll give you the keys." Wow, I can't believe this; how can this be? It turns out the solution was sleeping right beside me all along! I end up chauffeuring others around all week, including my roommate. When I tell this to the car full of people who picked me up, they say, "She manifested it!"

Turns out the entire week is one made up of these kinds of magical manifestations. At the end of the retreat, I casually mentioned the various bus transfers and the long wait I had in front of me; the woman sitting next to me offers to drive me to my airport motel, even though it's way out of her way. We have a wonderful time together.

This Kundalini retreat showed me how these kinds of last-minute surprises come from a place that knows more than I do. That place just manifests what's needed in the moment. I'm back to Basic Trust.

Chapter 6: Days of Sacred Wonderment

It Begins

Back at home, I come across an email announcing a Spiritual Symposium that is to be held online. I decide to just take a look at the topics. Nothing much of interest; but then one title makes me stop, "Sacred Mediumship." I don't know why. I don't even believe in this sort of thing. But now, my mind is flashing images of past occurrences, times when people who were dying, or had just died, had come to me energetically. I actually experienced their energy at that time and sensed what was going on.

Once, I happened to look down from my nineteenth-story window and saw a young man lying below, who had just committed suicide. Another time I viewed a man who had jumped from a tall building. Both times, I somehow knew what these people were thinking; mostly they were confused. They had no idea of what had just happened to them, or even that they were dead. They do not know where they were. I sent them energetic support.

Another time, while I was exercising on the bedroom floor, a relative who was dying of cancer, energetically dropped into my awareness. He was looking for companionship and support. Magically, a few hours later, I received a call asking me to come and sit with him, his hospice worker had been called away. I stayed with him until he passed away peacefully later that day.

Gee, maybe I should check this mediumship thing out. I am up for some new stimulation. Plus, by this time on the journey, I know how strange things appear just when the time was "right." So, I sign up for the Sacred Mediumship Course given by Suzanne Giesemann.

◆ ◆ ◆

I'm on fire! I'm going through the modules quickly. I learn Suzanne's "BLESS ME method." It's so easy to go into the higher frequency to receive "loved ones" and spirit guides for the "sitters," the persons for whom I am reading. I realize this mediumship experience is actually taking me into dimensions and frequencies that I've *already* been experiencing for years!

I ask friends to be my guinea pigs as I practice giving "readings." I'm rather nervous. I have no idea what to expect. But, yow, my first few practice sessions leave my mind reeling: A man of Buddhist lineage comes through and tells his daughter-in-law how much he loves her, and that he is here to guide her in her life. A beautiful young child materializes and tells her parents what it's like to be in heaven. A woman who had recently committed suicide comes through to apologize for her mistake. An alcoholic mother comes through and keeps asking her daughter, "What about those nightgowns?" Finally, I ask the daughter what her mother is talking about. The daughter says, "I don't know. I got rid of all my mother's things. But I do have a few of her nightgowns." So, I silently ask the mother, "So, what about those nightgowns?" She responds directly to her daughter, "When you wear one of those nightgowns, I will know you have begun to forgive me."

Well, at this point, I've done a bunch of readings. I'm amazed, flabbergasted at what I am learning about life on the other side. Some of the readings bring forth loved ones who had passed. Many readings bring in a spirit guide, who comes forth to deliver a message to the sitter. For example, I did a reading for a woman who wanted to get in touch with her friend who had passed. She later sent me this note: "Thank you so much for letting me be so elegantly connected with him and his spirit. I felt calm and well held. It was wonderful to hear you give a description of what was happening, as you first shifted into a non-physical dimension and then took time to have the spirit arrive. I listened intently to his voice as it came directly through you. Thank you so much. I have been filled with the sweetness of the whole experience since our session. So good to know the connection is also cherished from the other side."

Transcripts of Readings

Mother to Daughter: This is a transcript of my speaking *as* the deceased mother talking with her daughter. At first the mother is tentative. It takes her a while to adjust to the reality of speaking from beyond the physical domain. We wait patiently. Then, the mother begins to talk directly to her daughter:

> Mother: *"Samantha, you know I never, ever, thought I would come and be with you like this. In my wildest imagination, I couldn't have thought of this. I couldn't have dreamed of this. Where I am is so far beyond anything that I could even fathom when I had a*

physical body. It's so different here. So calm. There is so much love.

"And I see things. It's just a completely different view. I did so want to come and talk with you and tell you how sorry I was that I had to leave, and also how much I loved you. Although I have to say that I had no inclination of what love could be in this much more expanded environment, in which I find myself.

"So, I may not be great talking in this way, but I want you to know that I even love you more. I look down and am so proud of you, proud of all that you do, proud of all that you accomplish. (Her vibration is increasing now.) More than that, I'm really proud of the pure-ness of your heart. I don't even understand how that happened; how you can be so loving and compassionate. I wish that I could have been closer to you, but the circumstances didn't really allow this to happen because of the feelings, because of family, because of beliefs that had been learned for generations, certain ways to think and behave. I was so encased in those notions, so confined to certain thoughts and behavior. I am so sorry for your pain and discomfort, and again for the circumstances that no one knew how to change or escape. Do you understand what I'm saying Samantha?"

Daughter: "Oh yes."

Mother: "Thank you so much. I wanted to tell you this. I just see things so completely different; it's like putting on a gigantic, gigantic pair of glasses, and seeing the world, the beauty, and the joy, and the magnificence, and the amount of information, and atmosphere that exists. It's truly amazing.

"And so, I am sorry that I could not make, or did not make, your life more enjoyable, more loving, more protected. I would like you to know that here, I am growing. I am learning. I am seeing in ways I never did before. And there are helpers here. It's like one of your Zoom calls. They are helping me zoom into you now. They are helping me zoom into other realms, other behaviors, other dimensions, and I am beginning to see how my own soul can learn and change and grow. I am so thankful for that.

"This is what I have come to tell you. And by the way, your brother is here also, but he is just listening silently. He wanted to be here in this reunion; but cannot speak. (The daughter starts to cry.) And so, we are here as family, here as love. We are here as growing and learning and expanding. And I want you to know that I am here with you. I can zoom down. I can take care of you. I am with you any time you would like me to be.

"In this new terrain, what I think becomes reality; we don't have to wait for something to happen like on Earth. So, if you call me, or want to connect with me,

you just let me know and I will be there. Is that OK with you?"

Daughter: "Oh, yes."

Mother: "Thank you so much. Thank you so much. Is there anything you want to ask or say before I go?"

Daughter: "I miss you so much."

Mother: "Yes. Yes."

Daughter: "Do you hear us talking about you every day?"

Mother: "Yes, and this is one reason I wanted to come, for you to see that I am still here. My body is no longer, but my spirit, I am alive. I am with you. Even though you can't see my form, I am living, and I am loving, and I am connecting with you. Please remember that in your physical form."

Daughter: "And I'm glad you're in peace."

Mother: "Yes, unbelievable. I am so happy that I could come in today, even though it took me a while." (Mother and daughter are both laughing.)

Now mother and brother retreat. We thank them for coming.

Young Adult to Parents: This reading takes a bit of explanation; it is a second reading for these parents. During the first reading, their child came through at the young age at which she had passed. This time she surprised her parents by coming in as a young adult. She talks to her parents about her personal journey and to tell them what heaven is like. These are the words that the daughter speaks directly to her parents. (Note: I had to modify just a tiny little bit, in order to facilitate greater understanding for the reader.)

Daughter: "Mom, Dad, last time you welcomed me and allowed me to connect with you. You let me sit on your lap. It was an incredible experience for me. Somehow, because of your openness, I am now able to come back to you on a new level. I wanted to come back and inform you as to what is happening on this level, and maybe shed some light, from this frequency, to light up some of your deeper understanding as humans who still have bodies.

"I want to say, before I forget, that when you pass into this eternal realm, in which you already actually exist, I will be waiting for you, and I will appear to you at whatever age you wish, as a young child, as an eighteen-year-old woman as I am now, or from whatever will come our way. But I wanted you to be a part of this angelic process.

"After I came to you, I went to visit a girl through this medium. She was ten-years-old. And I think it was almost too much for her. I really realized that I needed to develop beyond my childhood stage.

"And I want you to know what it's like once a person passes. There are different areas, frequencies, dimensions, that the living soul goes to, depending on their life in a body, and how much they have learned

to see who they actually are. I wanted to come back so you can see that part of you, now, is this spiritual part. It is the deeper part of who you are.

"What happens when you come here, no matter what level, there are others that help you. And there's a continuation of growth and support that is unending. My helpers and guides also have helpers and guides. And there are those who are still numb and can't wake up; but they too will be helped.

"Heaven is very much like it is on Earth. There are things to do, and it's all toward the greatest good. It's all toward service for humanity, for God. We all are learning and developing and growing.

"I have blossomed because of your un-entrapment. It's like you released me, and I now wish to work with teenagers, to help them understand. It's very sad to look down and see the world, and the human race, caught up in this ego perception, separation and war-like stance. So, I wish to work with teenagers who are just starting to have their place, their opportunity, their exuberance, their creativity, their potential to see higher, deeper dimensions of themselves. And that is what my work is becoming.

"I was hoping this would not be a shock to you or a let down because I want to keep you abreast; I want to let you know what is happening with me. And I want to know and see what is happening to you.

"That is what I came to say today. I love you so much, and the love that comes in this dimension, in this frequency, there is nothing in the human vocabulary that can describe the unity and the magnificence of this space. That is what I've come to say. But before I leave, is there anything you want to ask, please?"

Mom (crying): "I'm still so sad about all the pain you went through."

Daughter: "That suffering is what allows me to have this magnificence; that suffering helped me be where I am. I would suggest you understand sadness and grief, and let these emotions wash through. They are no longer needed. I love you Mom."

Mom (crying): "I became a doctor because of you. I thought if I could help someone else…"

Daughter: "So, you see the Spiritual Law. Your pain brought you to serving in a way that you are helping others. You are doing something that makes a difference."

Mom: "People used to say that you had an understanding in life that was beyond your years."

Daughter: "I have had many lifetimes, but this one is so precious because I get to be with you. I had not been able to come through and talk like this, which is the wish of every spirit. We are still alive, and yet the human field, the human barrier, usually will not open to allow us to be heard. So, you both are a gift, not only to me, but to the human race."

Mom: *"We always thought that you were the gift."*

Daughter: *"Thank you. I'm going to be leaving now. I bless you both."*

Things Start Escalating for Me

For a few years now, I've had what I call "the Guys" come into my subtle awareness. They are sort of like ascended masters living in the highest realms. But this morning they sent me a direct message:

"You can be your own medium."

"WHAT? You're telling me that I can bring in my own guides!"

"Yup."

I'm astounded. But over the next days and weeks, I find that my guides are correct.

Many Guides

Now, all kinds of guides are flooding into me. So, I'm going to look at my journal entries. I'm going to take stock and sort them out in my head:

Arnold was the first guide to appear. He reminds me to relax. He tells me when to slow down and stay present. Jeremy came next. He instantaneously brings me knowledge, truth, and a certain kind of knowing. He helps me discriminate what's actually going on moment to moment. Mary is here too. She's lovely. She enters with a divine love and compassion, always here to comfort, illuminate, and say, "You are loved." Jerome teaches an important skill. He tells me to just be silent, wait during my readings. He says that the magnetic energy system will draw in any information needed in a reading. As I write this, I realize that these guides have been here all along; but I was too constricted and oblivious to perceive them.

◆ ◆ ◆

Wow, I'm on my morning walk when my first husband, who died so many years ago, makes contact. He whispers, "I love you," I just sob. I've been wanting this contact for years. I realize he has been with me all along, providing love and guidance throughout our courtship, marriage, and parenting partnership. I also know that he died at an early age in order for me to break out of my usual limited perception and discover the expansion that is meant to be. I thank him. This again brings tears.

Enter the Big Ones

I'm walking in the hall and Archangel Michael descends! I sense his huge wings against my back, supporting me. Whoa, this is the same kind of support that I've been feeling for a few weeks now.

A powerful metal rod runs down through my body, providing strength. Healing. I'm astounded. I remember to ask Michael for some kind of proof that this is truly him; the way I was taught in the mediumship course. He tells me there will be a sign. I run in and tell my husband that I just met Archangel

Michael out in the hall. (By this point he's not surprised by much.)

A few hours later, I log into the next lesson of my Sacred Mediumship course. It's Suzanne talking about how Archangel Michael came to her! She spends the next hour detailing an incredible story of how she received evidence, which confirmed beyond a shadow of a doubt, that Archangel Michael had indeed visited. This coincidence was quite enough proof for my own encounter in the hall.

◆ ◆ ◆

This morning, while meditating, I ask my guides what I am to learn today. The letters h-o-r appear. I get the hit. This is Thor! He says, "You always were a bad speller" (which is true). His huge overarching power comes thundering through with a message from the Cosmic Universe. "There is Inner light, Strength, and Protection." I'm in wonder.

A few days later, I meet yet another guide.

> I see diaphanous, transparent shapes, circles, triangles and squares intersecting, but not interfering, with one another. A huge cosmic eraser is annihilating any thoughts of my life in the past or in any past lives. I discover a point of Existence manifesting ongoing, endless, Reality. I sense a presence walking within me. Is this a past life, or something else? What is manifesting right now? A person appears, walking along a path. He looks and feels like Jesus.
>
> But how can this be? Yet somehow, I am this same person, with long robes and bare feet. I smell old sweat

and dirt as my flowing garments ripple in the breeze. What is happening? Yikes, I was just seeing diaphanous, transparent, shapes and now I am walking with-in Jesus!

Well, I've seen everything now, or maybe not.

I AM HERE Arrives

With pen in hand, I ask my guides what I'm supposed to discover today. Immediately this IMMENSE PRESENCE descends and starts to speak:

"I AM HERE to deliver a message to humankind."

An undeniable power floods in, completely filling the atmosphere. This power infuses, overpowers, and dissolves everything. There is nothing here but this enormous Power and Supremacy. This is some sort of Ultimate Source of Service, and It's raining down in the form of the manifested world! My body is vibrating. I am dumbfounded, engulfed in wonder as I experience an almost unbearable Love and Compassion creating the human race.

*I AM HERE speaks: "**Love is the way of the universe, the circuitry that connects as One Unfolding**. Human Consciousness is rising, evolving. Awake. See. Feel. Be. Act as my Will, my Heart, fingers and toes. Go forth and provide, deliver. I am the Way. **You are part and parcel of the Way. Come forth. Show yourself.** Be as you are, pure and safe and precious."*

I sputter, "How do I come forth?"

*"**Be your True Self. Be the Connective Web**. Feel it in your body, your surroundings, your soul. **Pray to this perspective and it will shine forth**. Follow our lead, follow your True Nature."*

My body is now jerking all around. I feel all shaky inside. It seems like big chunks of beliefs and old certainties are falling away.

*"Your body is being prepared to receive more light, more voltage. Observe. Flow with the 'Yes' of life as we prepare your soil. Focus, still and steady, on the way, the path. You are loved and protected. **Go forth, give, contribute, participate with Light. You are truly loved**."*

I must say this delivery is over-powering. I am in awe of what I just witnessed, encountered, and experienced. I'm a bit overwhelmed and will wait and see what develops in the next few days.

Space Cruiser Wormhole

I'm sitting here just meditating; but then, **I realize the entire universe is breathing!** I grab my pen.

The in-breath ushers in pure essence, a flowering of consciousness, an opportunity for growth and complete awareness. The out breath is cleansing the universe of all negatives and debris. My inner experience is radiating out in the shape of a cross; light is jutting out horizontally through my shoulders and arms; light is running vertically up and down my neck and back.

The light expands, grows, becomes immense. At the midpoint of the cross, a deep, deep wormhole appears. Wait, it's turning into a flying space vehicle! There's propulsion, movement. Now I'm zooming through space. I'm being tossed around, rolling like a tumble weed through open air.

I ask my guides, "What's going on?"

"You, we, are a Starship looking through the window of Becoming. We are traveling within, what you humans would call "history," a tumbling kaleidoscope of transpiring Evolution. This is God's spaceship, all swirling into multi-dimensional worlds, universes, dimensions, frequencies, manifestations, and yet, you see that all is One.

"This is God's playground, Source at Core, playing, practicing, evolving towards the greater Good. We pass through intermittent clouds, human debris, bloodshed, hardship, pain, determination and advancement. All swirls equally, a quantum soup, bubbling, fermenting, ready to give birth yet once again.

"We are here to journey with you. We are equals, as your human language would express. We are all God's creatures, handiwork, traveling at an unbeknownst

warp speed, silently, invisibly, merging, mixing, twinkling, and twisting toward a greater and greater evolutionary Reality. **This Reality, as the One Living Being, is to be shared as It buds, grows, and blossoms forth in strength, integrity, love, joy and peace.** *Do you understand?*

"We take you on this space journey today to show you how wormholes work. Just squeeze through the tiny hole that is pulling you towards your center—Universal Reality. **Look behind the surface, get to know the powerful, dynamic, all-knowing, ever-renewing energy, which fuels all Life. You are this life, this fuel, as are we.** *The ride is bumpy and arduous, but you will weather it and prevail. Keep your eyes ahead, focus your internal and external vision on Point Zero, the Oneness of Life Itself."*

"OK. OK. I hear what you, say," I chirp. "But this is so new, I'm a bit confused. I don't know where I am. There are no signposts here, and actually I don't want there to be signposts. Just give me a moment...."

I pause and experience. This is a place/space of grandeur and silence. Black velvet nothingness is moving and doing Its thing. I am Its thing. You are Its thing. This is Its thing.

So interesting. Just want to marinate in this movement, this subtle, s l o w, swirling, activating agency. This seems like the inner workings of time and mystery. This experience is scorching my mind.

Evidence in Readings

I'm fretting about my spiritual readings because I do not get the kind of evidence that my mediumship course teaches, like someone's birth date or where they live. My guides come in to confer.

> *"Remember, you have an immense team of guides, all wanting what is best for you—for the spirit that comes in, and for the sitter. We will not let you down. Trust in what comes to you currently; it is correct and true.*

> *"Don't be afraid to give the details of what you see. When you feel chaos or violence, speak to what you see happening. For example, you feel chaos, but you also see a man, a uniform, and people running upstairs. Say what you see out loud to your sitter. Speak confidently of what comes. In this way the spirit, which has chosen to come in will be heard correctly, and the sitter will be unburdened.*

> *"Remember you are an intricate part of the interconnected web. Don't confine your readings to your usual mind, to what you've learned or are learning. Blend completely with the Totality that occurs. As you know, you are in a higher frequency as you read. You can rest assured that what is needed comes.*

"Your readings are fine. You do not need to wonder or worry if the information is "real" or where it is coming from. Just BE what comes. Don't worry about the evidence, don't try. Your sitters know the answers in their heart.

"You are learning beautifully. We have chosen you for your ability to interpret what we are saying and to teach. It takes practice and time (they chuckle a bit about the concept of time) to hone your new medium skills. Relax. Don't fret. Get over it.

"You sure have a hard head. You need to accept the fact that you are one with us now—a blend— remember! Be with us. TRUST. We are showing you the way."

My Everyday Awareness Starts to Shift

*Walking along the bay, I'm floating in a vast field of existence. At the same time, I feel my feet firmly on the sidewalk. I notice **I am looking at the world through transparency**. I'm aware of a place where there is a split between my upper and lower perception. Higher awareness trumps lower.*

I notice my fishermen friends waving at me. They're yelling, "Good morning." I wave back, still in sort of a daze. I turn back to walk. Immediately, in that very second, my garbage man friend is beside me. He honks his horn at me every day. But today, his truck is stopped up along the curb, right beside me. I stop. He climbs down from his truck. We stand and face each other. It feels like we both want to hug, but don't. We speak for a few friendly moments and then continue on our way.

*As I continue walking, **I feel the world blossoming into utter bliss. I melt into Oneness. "Being" displays its Light show.** Different frequencies and levels of conscious awareness are streaming in. Sound, and form, also express themselves through a shared unified field, which manifests as the density of the Earth. This entire experience is surreal. Wow, now **I experience how sentient beings, worms, fish and sidewalk, are all of the same substance.** This is all amazing.*

◆ ◆ ◆

Everything seems to be going along fine, until one day I discover a huge bump in my journey. It stars out innocently enough.

Generational Abuse

I'm feeling sort of lethargic and down this morning. Strange. I meditate.

A warrior guide sits down beside me, relaxed and comfortable, "Don't worry," he says, "You have a deep fathomless reservoir of love and compassion. Now it's time to go in and deeply explore; and don't get caught up in the trap of ego. I will be your guide."

I realize I am in a quite a fog; it's all murky. The malaise begins to lift. Now, I'm drifting into a deep feeling of love. The warrior tells me, "Go inside. Watch. Wait. I will be with you." A huge, expansive, inter-connected web forms. My usual me-ness disappears. Suddenly, I have the intention to explore issues with my dad. I'm right here, right now, with no loss of focus or diversion. I'm in this wide-open field. I ask all my guides to help.

And then it happens: I feel like vomiting. I feel love, and at the same time, I smell a rotten stench. A little angel appears, dirty, wings all gray and smelling of bird droppings. Something is rotting, festering. Yuck, it's a rotten pool of muck. Images of my grandmother's basement come again and layer after layer I begin to understand things I never knew.

Images of ancestors descend. I suddenly see three to five generations who struggled with sexual abuse. I smell the stench of forgotten children, forgotten victims. Nobody is talking! Everyone pretends they do not see the forbidden. I realize the sexual behavior with my father started so young that I never knew, didn't remember. But now it all comes tumbling through.

My Dad used me to play out his own childhood sexual trauma. I get a picture of my father being abused by his mother, my Nana! I am shown that my dad's mother was sexually abused by her father, and her mother (my dad's grandmother) was also abused.

Yikes. I'm so hurt, so embarrassed, so betrayed. How could my father do this to me, and his mom do it to him, and on and on?

Another wave, I'm feeling filth again. I'm going to vomit. I'm outraged. But I'm focused, a warrior. I dive right into the muck! My hands are slimy. "Be gone. Be gone." I'm weeping and pulling out yards and yards of bloody, slimy, evil crap—pulling the lines back through generations. "Be gone. Be gone."

I take all these gory lines of filth and muck and set them on a huge fire, the way they burn corpses in India. I throw all these cords of gunk into the fire, along with all the bloody, slimy wounded tissues and residue.

My nose curls in disgust. I watch the fire. But this gunk doesn't want to be burned! I hear myself saying, "No, no, the hate, the evil, has gone on long enough. Now it's time to love." Instantly, a deep, open, infinite space emerges. I think I need to stop now.

That night, when I go to bed, I ask my guides for clarity and verification of what is being revealed.

◆ ◆ ◆

The next morning, I hear a voice saying, "Leviticus 2:12."

This must be from the Bible, with which I am very unfamiliar. I look it up. I do some research and find the following: "Bring to the LORD an offering of the first fruits; they are not to be offered on the altar as a pleasing aroma." "There is a moral requirement, a sacrifice to be made in the first harvest. It goes against God to participate in this harvest for pleasure."

This is the confirmation for which I asked! This tells me that it is against God's nature for parents to use children for sexual pleasure. But I get the feeling that I haven't seen the entire picture yet. I ask my guides to answer a series of questions about what is yet to be revealed. They answer with a "yes" or "no" to most of my questions and confirm the abuse.

> *"None of the perpetrators in your family was ever confronted by the family, and none of the victims ever received acknowledgment or support. They had to go it alone, and hence generational karma grew in intensity. It has stopped with you. There is still more to come, but it's not yet time for you to know."*
>
> *I am sobbing with shame, sorrow and hurt. My heart is broken. I feel used for false purposes. I'm experiencing damaged tissues, submerged, and hidden imprints, the result of this generational abuse, and abuse rendered by all abusers on all souls.*
>
> *Now, somehow, all souls who have been abused, past and present, come together.*
>
> *I silently whisper, "May we gather in this like frequency, bind, unify, and release."*
>
> *Together, all of us breathe, release, relax and rejoice in harmony. We are cleansing and releasing past Karmic impressions and influences. This feels good.*

Yahoo Arrives

The next morning there's a frequency arising that wants to be explored. My body is jerking all around. This frequency is amorphous, alive, moving, fluid. It is waking up! Dancing, saying "hello."

It speaks: "Bet you never saw us before." (This is certainly true. This is unimaginable.)

"Well, imagine it, baby, cause we're here." (This spirit is feisty! It wants to move, dance and jump around.)

I ask, "Could you be a bit of trapped energy that's freeing itself?"

"You bet, sister; we've been trapped and silent for so long and now we are here to yell, yip, laugh, dance, pray and rejoice."

"Did I actually help you come? Talk to me. Who are you?"

"We give new life, new energy, to the Universal System of Good. Just call us 'Yahoo!' We love you. We love all. We are here now to assist in your quest to free blocked energy. And we know more than thee. We can help whoever comes into contact with us. Yahoo! We are overjoyed. You can't believe our joy, our love, our happiness."

"I know, I'm just beginning to see it now. It's actually hard for me to believe."

"This has nothing to do with belief, sister; this is Love pure and simple—unleashed and made available for Good."

"How did this happen?"

*"You opened yourself up to see the lock-up of your own energy due to generational abuse. You witnessed how generations of abuse have caused harm and led many humans astray. You allowed yourself to go into the muck and slime. We thank you for your work. We luxuriated as you helped to set us free. We thank you yet again. **This helps all of humanity.**"*

I am still speechless. Here is all this jubilant energy dancing around, talking, communicating and I'm frozen. I don't know what to make of it all.

"Oh, just relax girl, loosen your bra. We will help you ease into this newly released, expansive energy, the energy which is yet to be born in you. You just relax, observe, wonder. Be, and we will be with ye. See, that's how old we are; we use words like ye."

"I am so grateful you are freed. Your love and joy will help us all. I am so happy that you've revealed yourself to me. Now I'm going to just rest in this silence, emptiness, and peace. I see this expansive emptiness is free, and it's me! I bow."

Personal Abuse Revealed

I ask my guides, "What am I to learn today?"

I just sit in emptiness and listen. I'm catapulted into an amazing, total, BLACK DEPTH. There is security. I see that I have a magnetized center, which attracts answers, information, and healing.

> *A deep voice says: "This is a frequency pattern, which is to be healed. It holds deep, troubling actions that have crippled human functioning for decades. There are burdens of accumulated stress, dis-ease, abuse, and ignorance here. This is a frequency of putrid, repulsive patterns, behaviors that go against the purity of the soul, your soul. It is good for you to ask, inquire, and feel into the totality of this frequency domain. We ask that you do this now. We are with you."*

> *Instantly a thought of my father comes in. I stop. I don't want to continue. Can this be? Where will this lead? But I know my guides are with me, lending a layer of support and comfort—and they are asking me to be completely open right now to this frequency. I Pause, watch and listen.*

Caution: If you are a victim of abuse, what you are about to read, may trigger feelings of anxiety, depression, trauma, panic, shame or rage. What comes next is very raw, but I include the actual frequency of this experience to shed some light on the true innocence of those who have been abused. If you struggle with abuse issues, please allow an experienced professional to help you release energies that may yet be frozen.

♦ ♦ ♦

My father is standing with me. He is nude, I am small, probably—5 or 6 years old. He is acting all soft and happy like, wanting me to come be with him. Something makes me uncomfortable, uneasy, but I love my Dad and go to him. He lifts me up and hugs me. I love to be up against his body and have him hold me close. I'm also wondering why he has no clothes on. He lays me on the bed and sits down beside me. He puts his hand on my stomach and then moves it down to my crotch. He does it gently and sort of hums. This is strange, unknown behavior, but it feels good—soft and gentle like. I close my eyes. When I open them, I look at Dad's face. He looks down, I look down and I notice his thing is big. I've never seen it like this before. I'm mesmerized. I can't believe this could be. He asks me to touch it and I do. It's soft and hard at the same time. I feel some kind of movement, awakening, down by where his hand is rubbing.

I tell my guides this is about as far as I'd like to go today. They understand and I discontinue this inquiry and distract myself on the computer. This is a very heavy realization.

Purple Saves the Day

I have been walking, meditating, and inquiring about the abuse situation for days. This morning, during my usual walk, the color purple enters. What is this?

I feel into the clear, viscous, purple gel coating my body. It's alive; it has its own language! I am swimming in purple. I shift into a non-physical dimension. I allow whatever wants to unfold to have its way. I wait.

Suddenly I'm in a higher domain than I have ever been. This is completely new territory, new terrain. I'm like in my own tiny space cruiser, zipping around, touring. Somehow, I know this terrain of pure, clear, white empty space; it has hints of other worlds and other dimensions.

This is all happening within my physical body, which is now enormous! I'm buzzing around, flying through an internal landscape. This is amazing, incredible!

I realize that the deeper I am able to explore, the more Reality is shown to me. This makes all the yucky stuff that comes up seem like a gift.

Crunchy Resistance Shows Up

Bam, another shift.

All of a sudden, there's tension and a crabby knobbiness at the base of my spine. It's all boney, crunchy, jagged, crushed, and annoying. Now, I witness a strange thing: Purple (P) and Crunchy Resistance (CR) are "facing off." I listen:

P: I'm here to love you.

CR: Well, I am here to resist. I hate you; don't come near me.

P: I still love you. I am patient, soft, free.

CR: Oh yeah, well I am hard and determined. I've been doing this for years. I can out-wait you.

P: We know it was necessary for you to become hard and crunchy. You are free to feel your crunchiness, knobbiness, resistance, tension and pain. Go right ahead.

CR: You're just trying to trick me, so I'll relax and come over to your side.

An image of my Dad comes up. Wow, I'm morphing into sexual feelings for my Dad as my 5-year-old self. This is the bandwidth in which I was caught, trapped! This is the part of me that is hard and crunchy. I revert and go inside more deeply, guarding my young self to any outside influence. I'll just stay inside, encased, protected, alert. I will go softly through life by myself. People won't even know; they don't care anyway.

But wait, things are morphing again. Now, I'm swimming in purple. I allow. I step outside of the hidden-child-self and look down. I'm mesmerized. There is deep, soft pleasure. No more unconscious fear, guilt, and shame! How did this happen? What does the color purple have to do with it?

I look it up: Purple stands for awareness, knowing, universal identity, and connection to all that is. There are no "issues" in this vibration. I thank Purple for coming.

◆ ◆ ◆

Spirits Speak Directly to My Sitters

I'm super busy with my spiritual readings now. I'm doing over twenty readings a month, from around the world. A few "super spreaders" have really spread the word. It's great.

I love the readings I do with my sitters; what comes through is so diversified and real. But here's the thing, magically, every time, the words of the loved ones, or guides, come directly out of my mouth! The spirits are the ones who talk directly to my sitters. This is not what the mediumship course is telling me to do. So, I'm still wondering why the spirits' words come directly out of my mouth. My course teaches that mediums *describe* details to the sitter. *Mediums do not talk as the spirit itself.* But this is what is happening to me.

The spirit, who comes through in a reading, usually asks the sitter if he or she would like to talk directly, gets a "yes," and then proceeds to engage directly with the sitter, with their words coming out of *my* mouth. Sometimes the spirit refers to me as "this woman." One time when I thought the spirit had receded, the sitter and I began talking; the Spirit interrupted and said, "If this woman would stop talking, I have something more to say." (This was pretty funny.)

◆ ◆ ◆

Well, I've conferred with both a shaman and an experienced medium, who was recommended by Suzanne, about my problem. They told me that I have a "gift." Some of my sitters have said the same. This is difficult for me to accept; it's almost as if I'm channeling. Channeling!

Well, I didn't believe I would ever travel *beyond* my personality. I didn't believe I would have *mystical* experiences. I didn't even believe in mediumship, or guides, or automatic writing. Now I think that this channeling thing is something I really need to check out. Channeling? Me? Could this be true?

Once again, a new frontier seems to have opened for me. I am eager to explore.

Chapter 7: A New World

For a few weeks now, I've been watching different channelers on the Gaia website.* It's fascinating, and I'm learning a lot. There is one particular channeler to whom I'm drawn, Georgia Jean. She channels "The Circle of Light," who I learn about from reading the book, *The Circle of Light and the Philosopher*. This book *talks about* an enormous, magnificent, beautiful ball of consciousness, which through *Its* wisdom, and vibrational energy, contributes to our life experience on Earth. I decide to explore further.

♦ ♦ ♦

The first thing I learn from the book is that the Circle of Light is a collection of "Light Beings," which consists of about twelve regular members, like Archangel Michael and Salvatore. They also have guests who visit, like Mother Mary and the energy of the Consciousness of Christ. That's interesting.

I wonder if these light beings are like the guides that come forth in my readings. For example, when I read for a young professional woman, she later wrote, "Our session together was terrific! At the beginning of the session, I was significantly upset about an incident at work. But then the Archangel Michael came through for heaven's sake! Towards the end of my session, I just felt completely calm, the sting of what had happened had been neutralized. I felt very peaceful and content. I am looking forward to my next reading." *Actually, I realize that I have already encountered these energies in my spiritual readings.* This is very encouraging. I continue to read.

The Circle of Light operates through members and guests who come together collectively in a sort of "inverted disco ball." Each member beams its energetic "light wisdom" into the center of the circle. In this way, their collective wisdom-energy combines into just the right thing, for the right moment, at the right time, for whomever they are serving. Sounds good to me. Think I'm going to continue to troll for insights and concepts that resonate at this point.

What Resonates

Consciousness doesn't come to Earth to just "hang out." It's here to learn, grow, expand, try out different experiences and various "life games" like warrior, detective, guru, scientist.

We humans exist as a multi-dimensional experience. We are far more than what meets the eye of our usual, limited, perceptions. Although we habitually focus on our three-dimensional (3D) form; we also exist on the fourth, fifth, sixth, seventh, eighth, ninth, tenth, eleventh, and twelfth dimensions. This means we are also capable of focusing on past, future, parallel, and concurrent life experiences. (Yow, this explains why, over the years, I have experienced so many various dimensions—from the usual 3D ego perspective of bewilderment, anxiety and confusion, to encounters with 5D experience, like bliss, knowing and illumination. It also explains experiences of past lives, finding myself in collective realms and going on "magic carpet rides." Now, I'm really listening to what the Circle of Light has to say.)

We humans have "superpowers." We are actually "the vanguard of the experimental edge, always trying things on." **We are part of a "co-creative"** *collective* **experience.** (This is how we are able to tap into various "band-widths," like I did with my experiences of sudden death, the 9/11 attack, and the realm of childhood abuse.)

As humans we have the power to choose. Thoughts and feelings are not good or bad; they are just energy-forms. These energy-forms will naturally move to higher vibrational fields, *if we have the intention* to move into higher vibrational experiences. Experience of "ascension" means the dissolution of identification with human forms. It means we need to allow our physical form to fully embody our expanded soul consciousness. (This is what I am just beginning to truly understand and want to know more.)

We humans are so powerful, **we have created a "resistance wall" in the collective social consciousness of humanity**. This "dam of resistance" holds us away from our true, expanded, experience. **Resistance has a purpose.** It creates the dense form in which we humans live, but it also is what keeps us bound to our usual, familiar, perspectives. **Energetically, we humans resist the fact that we are the size of an ocean**; we are actually much more than our tiny drop of physicality on Earth.

If we **want our higher minds to reign supreme, we need to stand and face whatever arises in our experience.** The Circle of Light tells us, "Don't fight it or change it. Just acknowledge the experience and let it move on." In this way, we release trapped energy and have access to new "creative" energetic powers.

The Circle of Light tells us that we humans need to learn to say, "OK, I am feeling sad right now, and I accept this resistance." If we get into a big struggle with our resistance, we will carry the burden on and on. Basically, **anything that pushes our buttons is reflective of something that we are still holding onto energetically, unconsciously, either from other lifetimes, or from our suppressed memories in this lifetime.** (This is the kind of thing that happened to me during my Snickers bar and Red Suitcase incidents. There are still times I go into suppressed, unconscious, energies. I want to learn the more effective response, "OK, I'm feeling x right now and I accept this.")

When our usual identity is freed up, our slowed-up energy can return to its original source. This is where simple Oneness occurs where there is a sense of Knowingness, a Oneness with everything. This is a deep internal feeling that recognizes the truth. In this higher frequency, questions simply disappear because we have no need to question.

We humans have the capacity to see deeper underlying light, color, and form. When we release our learned concepts of form, we can simply *become* vibration, color, and light. It's possible for us to connect, and resonate, with higher dimensions, higher frequencies, and even vibrational extraterrestrial beings. **What we humans see is dependent on the frequency from which we, ourselves, resonate.**

The Circle of Light tells us what human evolution is about. Our soul's expansion is what keeps pushing humanity's consciousness forward. Evolution is always happening; it manifests from a massive data-collection system at the heart-felt center of Love. Receiving is a matter of opening the portals of the heart, a matter of receiving what is already in creative existence. The higher we humans move up in dimensional fields, the more we contribute to the greater good, to the evolution of humanity as a whole. When we start to call in our natural powerful abilities, our consciousness will expand and our deep exploration will call forth "all that we really are."

◆ ◆ ◆

After reading *The Circle of Light and The Philosopher*, and recalling what I've been experiencing for years, I find I am really resonating with what they are saying. So, I've signed up for a session with the Circle of Light itself, channeled by Georgia Jean.

My first task is to prepare for the session. I think about what I would like to know and give the Circle of Light the following goals.

I am interested in deep healing and transformational work. My ongoing intention is to make the invisible world visible. I want to:

- Release trapped energy for all beings.

- Release deep-seated blockages that hinder full development.

- Release all unnecessary patterns.

- Heal early trauma from my nervous system in a way where all systems work organically, so that I am able to walk with comfort and ease.

Channeled Experience

I wanted to reset my nervous system to dispel trauma and lay a new neural pathway. I was told to RUN EVERYTHING through the heart; so, I worked on opening my heart using the infinity eight sign. I ran the infinity symbol through the back of my neck, at the base of the skull, then up through the pineal gland and down the back of my neck. I also ran the infinity eight symbol around my heart and thymus. (The thymus is behind the breastbone. I found it by feeling for the two pointy, center, bones located high up on my chest, right below my throat. Right below these bones lays the thymus.)

Next, I worked with resistance: The Circle of Light gave me ways to release energy from perceived blockages, old patterns, thoughts, feelings, and experiences of resistance. They had me run the infinity symbol around my heart and thymus and silently say, "I love and accept the part of me that creates this projection."

To access more consciousness, the Circle of Light suggested that, before going to bed, I carry the intention to manifest more of what I want. "I have the intention of accessing more neutrality, more love and acceptance in my daily life." The Circle also mentioned that we could learn more about our parallel lives, and past lives, in this way.

Finally, the Circle of Light instructed me to feel into my feet, to help ground me to planet Earth.

◆ ◆ ◆

All of this new information and experience is fantastic for me. I feel like I have been given a gift box of creative seeing and down-to-Earth tools, which I can incorporate into my everyday life. This new experience is opening me up in groundbreaking ways. It's as if a whole new frontier exists to be explored and tried out.

Deeper Understanding

It takes me a few days to assimilate the experience of my actual session with the Circle of Light. After some contemplation, and reflection, I come away with the following.

- Consciousness comes to Earth through the Heart. It anchors Itself to the fifth dimension; this is the new paradigm into which we, the human species, is growing. The Circle of Light comes from the highest dimension.

- It's through the Heart that Master Consciousness emerges.

- Be Anchored in the Heart at all times.

- Witness everything through the Heart.

- The Heart is what generates Reality beyond the old human paradigm.

- ANY thought, feeling, or experience is able to come through the Heart. By witnessing everything through the Heart, including collective energies, we can witness both Earthly Manifestation and the greater Knowingness.

- Whenever something comes from the 3D mind, from our usual human paradigm, I am to say, "I love and accept this projection."

- It's important to continually remember that the Heart *is* the master consciousness. I need to remember to surrender, to give over all my resistance to the "master." So, I plan on saying, "I give over the part of me which created this projection, this resistance. I created this, therefore, I can un-create this."

The Circle of Light explained that we come into the physical world with an "existence template." This template has a sort of skin which acts like a filter on our experience. This filter is what gives us a feeling of entrapment and restriction. This is the old human template which needs to be released, dissolved, and integrated. (This explanation corresponds to my notion of having trapped energy, which I've been feeling for years.)

When any energy is experienced around the existence template, we need to bring that energy into the heart and run it through the infinity loop; this is the way we humans can move into the new evolutionary template.

I realize that I use the belief that existence is being resisted, in order to resist. I use the feeling of existence being trapped in order to resist. I even use the experience of existence being trapped in order to resist. (Wow, this one really gets me.)

I need to surrender any sense of entrapment or restriction to the heart, to the master consciousness. I need to run everything through the heart and say, "I love and accept the part of me that resists."

◆ ◆ ◆

I've started to listen to the Circle of Light's recordings from the Master Consciousness Course, which Georgia Jean sent me. I love these recorded meditations.

Realizations of Master Consciousness

While listening to a Circle of Light recording, I choose to release and dissolve all mental and emotional stories. I choose to release all patterns of abandonment, heartbreak and loss. I ask to release and dissolve any original memories, and beliefs which are limiting the unfoldment from all my lifetimes—past, present, and future.

Suddenly, Michael, Mary, Solomon and Salvatore are swooping in to help. I feel safe. I feel loved. I feel my deep humanness. Some energies are beginning to release.

I choose to receive this new energy-consciousness as mine. *The field morphs, very powerful emotions are flooding in—fear and terror. I'm lost, I don't know where I am. There are no supports, just devastation, the very loss of existence! Oh my, now thoughts of death—the lid opening on my incubator, being lost in the national park, abandonment, my father—it's all flooding into my heart.*

Wait, there is a shift going on, now I'm receiving all this with grace! I say, "Enter, you are welcome. You are all loved and accepted. Please bring your energies here. Please do."

*I see there is sooo much energy tied up in my old panic. But now, my heart is an open center for metabolization. Yeah! Old baby neurons are triggering. I hear the whisper, **"You have renewed life! You are being dismantled, transmuted, disassembled."** I'm seeing new connections being formed. Cells are merging, firing in all directions— dancing and connecting. These too, I bring into the loving cavern of my heart; the energy is swirling like a whirlwind.*

Now, I choose to release any, and all, mental and bodily holdings, plus all programming and resistance that has been managing, or controlling, my creative energy. Wham. I see the old rubber-band connections that have been limiting me.

*I AM choosing to release all energies and memories from all past, present, future, and in-between realms. **I see the collective! I see all dimensions and levels**— now soothing the area of my pelvic base through a loving pink light, **simultaneously filling in, consuming, and birthing all.***

I visualize life's experience in the state of abundance and prosperity—bringing spirit and body together, living moment-to-moment in a truly embodied way, guided by the authenticity of Life—all coming from ground zero, from the Great Neutrality.

*Now there is a lovely green light flowing though my head—picking up any residual energy and washing it all down through my legs, out through the soles of my feet. **All experience is coming up to be re-loaded.** This may take me weeks to integrate!*

◆ ◆ ◆

During my morning meditation, I feel the ENORMOUS POWER that a human being actually has. As I experience this frequency, I choose to shift, to turn over all my familiar stories, body jerks, "the works," to the Master Consciousness of the Heart. Yow, there's bliss here, and confidence in the higher "Me." I feel extreme comfort, security, and confidence as I let go of my old control.

All possibilities for change are open. There's an infinite stream of Intelligent energy going on. True Nature is providing all Its Essential qualities—joy, truth, compassion, value, love. **Planetary Consciousness is grounding; it is supporting the exploration of illusions, old mind sets, and baked-in stories.** I can see how **my daily life gives me a place to actually practice an expanded Life.** All the great themes are here—war, inhumanity, disease, suffering, opposition, resistance, polarities, wonder, enlightenment and more. Maybe different aspects hold more meaning for me, than for you; that's fine. But we humans, after all this time, still have not yet learned to allow, listen, and commune with each other or the great beyond.

A Prayer

I would like every human being to realize that consciousness does not end at the edge of the body; there is so much more to explore. I would like every person to know that they are Essential, that they can only lose what is false, because what is Essential cannot be destroyed. I would like each person to accept the fact that life is not a bed of roses; it's not all light and love; that a true path is just what Life is. Life has its ups and downs. Sometimes we are clear; sometimes we are confused, but all is well-worth exploring.

So, I pray to God, True Nature, Being-ness, Life Force, or whatever you want to call it: "Why can't we just all move into the Greater Intelligence? After all, this Knowingness is already inside us. Why can't we just release our illusions of separation? God, can't you just speed things up?"

OK, OK, I see that I just went on a rant; but I do want to dissolve all un-needed programs, all old blueprints. I do want to dissolve the illusion of separation, invisibility, and resistance. Damn it, I wish there was a gigantic washing machine that could flush all the dirty water down the drain and start anew. Man, I'd better stop typing now and go make some breakfast.

This morning as I'm walking along the bay; **I actually sense the Collective Planetary Shift**. It's just like what the mystics and the Circle of Light talk about. We are moving from our old fear-based template to a new, freer, more creative template.

This shift is moving us into a full, authentic, expanded life—a Real Life!

The new template, the new blueprint, is dissolving some of my old stories; it's taking me into new, more alive, territory. This shift is life-enhancing! I want to make this paradigm shift my primary focus, which is much easier to say than do. I must not feed my old way of operating. I must focus on the greater totality of who I am.

Wait a minute, wait a minute, I can see that this "want/need/must" business is coming from my old blueprint. I have shifted once again.

The Evolutionary Shift

I'm experiencing that the shift in human consciousness is a really BIG DEAL. Over the years, I've had a sense of experiencing evolutionary frequencies, but now this is different—more immediate, intense, front and center. It could be I'm being activated by listening to the Circle of Light recordings about the evolutionary shift that's occurring for planet Earth and human consciousness, but now I'm actually experiencing it, and at this point I've learned to trust what comes to me directly.

I am shifting away from the outdated three-dimensional (3D) way of functioning.

I see that I have been unconsciously operating from this fear-based position for most of my life; it's as if fear has been embedded in the very DNA of humans and has come home to haunt us now.

Most of us humans have learned to suppress our emotions. We judge them as good or bad, frivolous or shameful; but we had no idea that *not* feeling our feelings would lock our energy down and eventually erupt into pain, dis-ease, and violence. Now we see there is a global crisis under way.

The new paradigm of energy is a Godsend; it is designed to move us away from our old fear-based operating system, where survival signals get triggered and nervous systems create experiences of tension and anxiety. Many of us are still very troubled by the habitual operation of this primitive paradigm.

The Circle of Light tells us that we humans are "un-conscious reservoirs of rich collective energy," which is evolving into the new operating system, the new template of consciousness. We are shifting into our fifth-dimensional (5D) way of experiencing life. This is a radically different, greatly expanded, multi-dimensional, way of being in the world; this is what I have been experiencing all along without even knowing it!

The gigantic shift in human consciousness templates is creating cracks in our primitive way of operating; it is also opening doors for us as individuals, and for humanity as a whole. The shift is taking us into a more creative Reality, where we have the opportunity to experience greater love and joy in our every-day lives. Many of us, however, are still unable to enjoy this multi-dimensional way of life.

The good news is that we have been given new tools to help us release our old thoughts, feelings, and beliefs. I am finding these tools include bringing everything into the heart and employing the infinity eight loop. These practices are helping me navigate to the up-dated, multi-dimension template of Existence. In this way I, and we as humans, can acknowledge and release our resistance. We can move through our anxious moments more quickly. We can act with courage and skill, if we so choose. We can live the Fullness that we are designed to be. This brings me great joy and optimism.

◆ ◆ ◆

It's raining this evening, so I'm walking in the hall, looking out at the city and the bay, when I get the download.

There's a theme. I see the pattern of my journey! It is SEEING, KNOWING and TRANSMUTING energy as it comes in! Wow, I also see the reason for my life—to MAKE THE INVISIBLE VISIBLE. This is what I have come to do in this lifetime. I've come to see the Truth of what's actually happening in deeper reality. I've come to understand life from a mystical and biological perspective. I've come to transmute old energy, cleanse it through the heart, and pump it out into the world anew.

I surrender everything through the heart. I run the figure eight infinity loop through my thymus and heart. I turn the whole process over to the master. It's as simple as that. I turn over all my mind's toys of distraction, pain, heartache, wounding, separation, lofty experience, and ignorance to be cleansed through the Infinite Loving Heart. New energy is freeing up old energy. This unlocks my deep-seated, centered, Knowing-ness.

*I feel Consciousness of Christ while my feet are right on the ground. **My Body Consciousness and Heart Consciousness come together.** I can run all this energy through the heart. ALL is He, is Me, just is. In this place/space all stories "good and bad" are loved, accepted, and surrendered to Heart-Consciousness. Wow, now I'm adopting a new brain. I'm integrating somehow, and I'm walking with ease.*

I am so very happy to receive, and experience, this sacred information. There is not enough gratitude in the world to express my thanks.

♦ ♦ ♦

Today, I'm walking towards the bridge. I realize ***my identity has shifted. I experience that I actually am a Light Being!*** And I'm right here on the physical Earth plane. I am no longer "Barbara." That was the limited "me" that brought me to this stage, the one that was confined by the old, usual, head/mind dimension. Somehow, ***I'm getting an entirely new operating system***.

I just let it be. I have no idea how this works; but I know it will be shown to me. I know this heart-system needs to be integrated. It needs to be embodied in the physical realm. This is brand new. I'm just hanging out in the silence, the agency, as it magically comes through.

♦ ♦ ♦

There are no instructions that come with the shift, so I decide to **bring my "light body" down into my physical heart. I never dreamed this could be done**. I put on my Master Captain's hat and take on a whole new perspective. My expanded perspective provides me with a whole new understanding of how to guide my light body on the physical plane. Plus, I notice I've got a load of kids on board. There's the doer, the thinker, the distractor and of course the constant analyzer and commentator. It's a good thing that this new vehicle is so expansive. My practice is to bring everything into my heart center with my new Master Captain's hat on. I stay tuned and just watch what happens.

◆ ◆ ◆

Now things have really changed. Master Consciousness just whispered to me, "You are to write a book."

I'm supposed to write a book! Yow, what am I going to do?

The voice responds, "Use your collection of journal entries."

Oh, thanks, that's a big help.

So, now I am no longer taking excerpts from my *past* journals, *I am journaling in* present time. It's a bit scary to share without having time to reflect or know where the book is going, but this is my learning edge so I'm going to do it anyway. I find myself writing non-stop.

◆ ◆ ◆

Besides writing all day, I realize that I've been dreaming every night, which is unusual. This morning I discover why— my master consciousness has been fostering, pushing, expanding, and preparing to find an embodied "seat" within me, to go center stage so to speak. How do I begin to explain?

Wham. A great deal of buried fear pushes its way in, as I lay in bed, seemingly relaxed. Waves of deep subtle fear come again and again and again, with no known cause. I witness lifetimes of being alone, separate, abandoned. I pull the fear into my heart, knowing that this is energy asking to be released. On a deep level, I realize this separation is, in fact, not true.

*Master Consciousness now comes to the forefront. This time I invite Its Power. I am not afraid. I am learning to accept all my Power. I stay completely in the moment. Oh, **this is the "seat!" It's the Power of Continual Awareness; it's the power to be aware of this very moment, this ongoing-eternal-moment. It's the power of learning to let master consciousness do Its Work.***

*Whoa, now I'm sensing a deep bottomless well of potential, and It is walking! The potential is walking! Complete silence, Nothing-ness is oscillating, moving, expanding, evolving. **Nothingness is churning out ongoing nourishment**. I surrender.*

Sacrifice all to the Master, to the Kingdom. Just let all limitations be spun into possibilities. I am awash with gratitude. I throw everything into the cross that appears within my heart center. I throw everything

*into the flame to burn and purify. My old and new
"Self" bows to the Master for the greatest good.*

◆ ◆ ◆

This morning I'm wondering, why am I writing this book?
What am I trying to do?

I'm documenting the journey of the Self, the journey of the
Soul to find the Truth. This is the charge of All Humanity, of
all sentient Beings—to be totally Alive and Awake. **I want to
provide a window for those who are interested, to look
through and intimately see the journey of one soul**,
which in this case just happens to be mine. **I want to help
others see and understand the greater possibilities that
are available.**

Once again, I see that I am into "I want. I want." I'll use my
new tools and give all these wishes over to the Heart.

◆ ◆ ◆

Now I become aware of the brilliance, ingenuity, and
superlative creation of the "young me." I understand the
tenacity, the fortitude of the warrior who has brought me to
where I am. I surrender all to the Master Consciousness
Creator who has been creating all distractions, beliefs,
concepts, and stories of "me" all along. This Creation was,
and is, truly masterful.

*Now the Light, which previously had been experienced
from above, is downloading into a fully-open and
Expansive Heart. This Light Body brings into my
physical body all higher, deeper wisdom and
knowledge. Now there is a full "holding" of experience*

going on, it's divine, serene. This experience, this Knowing, anchors Me home. It anchors me in this moment. This is Its proper place—right here on planet Earth. Feels like my "eagle has landed." It's HERE.

Oh, now my old doer/helper pattern comes up again. It comes in as a distraction. I use my tools, "I love and accept the tenacious young me and I give her over to the master. I love and accept the part of me that still resists full mastery." I feel little points of resistance in the back of my neck and the base of my spine. I invite the Earth and its total powers to support this mastery.

Later, as I reflect, I realize the tools I've been given from the Circle of Light are changing my life. Running everything through the heart, using the infinity loop to purify the energy, working with resistance, are definitely enhancing my life. My everyday life seems easier, insights more immediate. Conscious integration is happening more quickly. I realize that I am now using these tools daily; sometimes they just start up automatically.

I wake up in the middle of the night, freezing, my hip is aching, I'm crying. Something is happening. I can't stop crying. I don't know why. Then I recall a friend saying to me, "You are writing a spiritual memoir." The word "memoir" somehow triggers me. It makes it sound like this book is about me. The book cannot be about me. It must be about the journey, the journey of the soul.

The book is about something much bigger—a gigantic energy, a beautiful force that is available to everyone; it's a force that comes through everything. This energy doesn't fit into just "me." I'm feeling angry right now; this is not the way the journey works. This Energy, this Force is MUCH too big.

◆ ◆ ◆

The next morning, I wake up early, crying. I feel terrible. I don't know what's happening. But this time, instead of analyzing, I leave it to master consciousness. I need help. The word "metamorphic" floats into my head. I don't know what this means. I get an image of a gigantic force trying to squeeze into a tiny hard rock-like space, like my ego self. This is not going to work. The rock is too hard; it's too small to accommodate this gigantic benevolent energy. I'm afraid, and grieving, at the same time.

I'm changing, molting, shedding old skin, peeling off an old shell.

I hear a whisper, "Don't fret about your book. Let everything come into your heart, into your Sky Consciousness."

I use my tools, "I love and accept the part of me that resists. I love and accept this resistance." This resistance is filled with eons of old, corrupted human energy. It wants to be drained; but doesn't know how.

Whoa, everything s-l-o-w-s way down. It's OK now, at this moment, to be in the unknown. The heart, the huge heart is big enough to allow, accept. The pressure eases somewhat. The infinity loop, yes, I run the infinity loop. I place the rock-like lump into my heart. There is fire! My old mind wants to go back, "I love and accept this resistance." This energy goes into the flame. There is so much old coal to burn; but the bigger "me," the "soul me," can do this! It CAN be done.

Later I looked up the definition of metamorphic: alteration of the composition or structure of a rock by heat, pressure, or another natural agency. I realize higher Intelligence uses prolific ways to get Its message across—thoughts, feelings, experiences, life circumstances, and definitions to name a few.

◆ ◆ ◆

This afternoon, while listening to a recording, the Circle of Light asks, "What currently holds a charge for you?"

God, it's this damn book! I'm writing from 5am to 5pm, and sometimes in the middle of the night. I'm obsessed, all wrapped up, entangled.

I pause to let things unfold. OK, OK, pull in all the energy involved in writing this book—perceptions, thoughts, creations, emotions, stories; bring it all into the sky-like heart.

Pull in the whole blinking primitive paradigm and purify it with the figure 8 loop. Purify all the templates, all the personal and planetary imprints, all the patterns and programs, everything that has created this story—of enlightenment, finding the prize, the Light, Home, God, the truth, the search. This is daunting.

OK, pause again. Take it all in and let it go.

Walking in the Kingdom

This afternoon the sun is shining. The birds are chirping. A butterfly almost hits me in the eye. I'm walking through the neighborhood garden.

> Suddenly, **I'm actually walking in the Kingdom!** The Kingdom! I've heard this word, but this is what the "Kingdom" actually feels like; it is what the kingdom is. Embodied! My light body has descended. My master consciousness is activated. It's walking!
>
> Dominion. Wow, this is what dominion really means— being fully awake, acting in conjunction with the Life Force, moving effortlessly through the ongoing moment.

I never dreamed that one day I would actually experience the meaning of dominion as a human being. I am astounded. Delighted. A new world is emerging. I give great thanks.

My Life Explained

OMG! I'm at the end of writing this book. This morning I was led to listen to a Circle of Light recording which explains what's been happening to me throughout my entire life! It puts my entire spiritual journey into a framework that makes complete sense, not just for me, but for humanity. I am so excited. Delighted. Overwhelmed, really.

I think I have to start at the beginning. The Circle of Light explains there is a major shift in human consciousness going on. Humanity has been moving from an old, primitive, un-conscious, fear-based paradigm to a grand, new, expansive, conscious paradigm. This radical new awareness is birthing a freer, more multi-dimensional expression of humanity. Yes, this is what has been happening for me. And I see how I've been seesawing between the two paradigms—old and new.

Now, I'm really paying attention to the recording. It explains, how for many years, I've been operating from my "known zone," the framework that was familiar and comfortable to me. In my old paradigm, I felt I was "unseen" and "misunderstood," so I kept quiet and went inside to hide. This fear-based paradigm, driven by primitive programming, has become imprinted into the human cellular structure and the collective world consciousness. Today, we don't even think about this ancient programing; we just continue to act unconsciously from this old way of doing things.

The limitation of the human Soul, the higher Self, has resulted in the suppression of our more expanded selves. We have learned to resist our natural feelings which are meant to be experienced and processed so that we can move on. The old paradigm taught us to label our feelings, as good or bad, right or wrong. The Circle of Light asks us to witness how we bypass our feelings, or stuff them down. This has led to a more violent eruption of shame, anger, fear, and aloneness on the planet. We now see violence happening on a global scale.

The problem here is that the old, suppressed, energy is coming up for a reason. It is pushing through to be seen by humankind. It is pushing through to be processed and transformed into new, clean, reusable energy that is readily available for all. The Circle of Light tells us, "There will be phases in your journey that threaten your mind, the same as if you were under attack in the cave. These survival signals emerge to make you take notice. They give you an opportunity to learn and expand. The nervous system that creates the experience of anxiety and fear is designed to give you experiences to work through in the game of life."

This reminds me of the fear that came up when I was lost in the national park, or the anger that arose when my husband didn't see my red suitcase. When I think of all the times I've been triggered, even by a little Snickers bar, I can see there is a tremendous amount of energy that is tied up in the old system. And that energy wants to be released. This is why my soul wants me to see and process my traumas instead of resisting them.

Wow, this is why I experienced trauma in the incubator, anger in the pool, and situations of abuse. This stuff is personal. I am grateful. I realize that processing these kinds of experiences has helped me move through more and more thresholds. Difficult experiences have helped move me into a more joyous expansion in my everyday life.

The Circle of Light explains that resistance is what keeps us in our maze. They say, as we begin to understand the "laws of resistance," we can viscerally experience a different way of life. The more we develop and explore, the more we will learn how to dissolve our resistance and go beyond the ego mind. The Circle assures us that the "personal work" we've done so far is not for naught. It is what allows us to receive the new, thriving, generating energy. When we truly move into master consciousness, we remove old, contracted, resistant, experiences of the primitive mind. Our old cellular system dissolves, and our expansion becomes phenomenal. Wow, this is how I feel. This is what I've been experiencing all along the way. As my ego mind recedes, my essential mind expands.

When higher consciousness begins to overtake my old way of seeing, my new perspective is no longer about being successful, feeling appreciated, or having people like me. It's about getting up at 3:00 am and writing. The new consciousness paradigm actually provides a new baseline, so that I am creating from a safer place, in my body, mind, spirit and community.

This is why I am no longer anxious about world events. I no longer need to turn away or put my head in the sand. I can respond from a calmer place, with less emotion, and more compassion. I am more resilient. This new expanded paradigm, *this new programming, actually is establishing a new baseline for me*. This brings my life into a new glorious experience, even when I judge things to be good or bad. Yes, my primitive mind continues to come up, but I don't get as hooked as I once did, or if I do, I usually am able to process the distress much more quickly.

The Circle of Light says, "Don't be mad at your mind, instead entrain your mind to work for, rather than against you. After a while, with practice, the mind will see for Itself that the new way is better. Your mind will learn to trust Its creative self. Then the process will become fun, amazing things will happen, synchronies will occur, and doors will open that you never knew about."

Yes, I have to admit that *learning to bring my brain down into my heart has greatly enhanced my life's perspective*. I can let go much more easily. I can run my distress through the infinity eight purification system. I can drop into my own energetic qualities of Self. I can tune into the collective, and into the vibration of what's happening. It really is all just energy. *I just love and accept whatever part of me that comes up. This is what I am learning to do. And hurray, I am seeing that it works!*

The Circle of Light says, "Soul Consciousness comes into human experience to keep us interested in what's happening. When the soul wants new experience, it will move you on to do new things. It says, 'what's the point of dying when there is so much happening right now. You don't have to die in order to re-incarnate.' To keep vitality in your life, just keep being open to possibilities of experience on this planet."

Lordy, this explains so much of why I've been led to go to some very unexpected places over the years. Running a motel in Arizona. Working with fashion models in New York City. Teaching cops human development skills. Becoming a clown. Taking Aikido lessons. All this experience was part of my journey. And who knows what the future holds?

It's Time

It's time to end this book. When I recall how I started this journey, I am truly amazed at what has occurred.

At the beginning I didn't even know that I was on a spiritual path, all I saw was a soul in agony after a personal tragedy.

Since that time, I have learned to go deep inside, explore with courage and steadfastness. My ego-self has begun to heal. Words of archangels and higher beings have come out of my mouth. I had no idea that any of this was possible. Emotional wounds have softened. I have traveled to the depths of collective agony, and the heights of mystical bliss, discovering that both wonder and grief have their gifts.

In spiritual readings, I have brought forth mothers, fathers, wives, children, and numerous guides for people who want to hear from those who are beyond this physical realm. Sitters have become my partners. This is because the spirits who comes forth, myself, and my "sitters," all contribute to the sacred mediumship event that occurs. There is great satisfaction knowing that I can use the spiritual awareness that has come to me to serve others more deeply; this goes beyond the usual teaching, counseling, and listening that I've been doing for much of my life.

Feedback from my readings has brought me much joy. For example, I did a reading for two people who had left their old country amid chaos. They never knew what happened to their mothers. After these readings, I received this note, "You are the greatest gift we could ever have gotten. The peace and beauty you brought to our lives through your mediation, letting us meet with our mothers again, cannot be expressed in words."

Now I find myself traveling, and co-creating with the ongoing flow, which has become my way of life—both ordinary and extraordinary. I've discovered that when I leave my window open, and allow Sky Consciousness full rein, the Magical Mystery can have its Way. I give great thanks for this.

While I used to think this journey was about me, I have come to realize it's about the journey of The One Soul, the same soul that is a part of you, me, and all humanity. I've come to see how each one of us plays a role, individually and collectively, in moving the consciousness of humankind forward. My greatest wish is that we shift into the New Operating Paradigm, into the Greater Good.

Final Whisper

In the end, the spiritual journey is about US, you and me, all of humankind. I'm now at my computer, listening to my guides as they speak.

> *"Please dear ones, continue your search to know who you really are, to discover your true potential as a human being. You each have the power to move humankind forward.*

> *"Do the best you can—little by little, bring everything, and we mean everything, down into your physical heart—all troubles, hate, fear, shame, distrust, dis-ease. Your heart consciousness is bigger than the sky. The consciousness of the heart is the actual place/space which can absorb all human trauma and distress. So, let the heart do its work.*

> *"Participate. Help the human race to clean up the river of hate and fear that flows beneath your current, collective, level of consciousness.*

> *"We have asked the human who is writing this book, to put our invitation into more human words for you."*

◆ ◆ ◆

There is a concrete skill behind all that's been experienced and revealed to me that I would like to leave you with. This is the most useful, and universal, skill that I have discovered on my journey.

Here is the skill: Take the content of your mind, bring it physically down into your heart. This takes practice. Deposit the content of your mind into your heart. This is where your Sky Consciousness, or Super Consciousness, resides. This Power that you have inside is the best single tool I can leave with you.

This skill, like any other, takes work and persistence. However, with practice, I've discovered that the capability to deposit things in the heart moves along with deftness. I'm finding, with practice, this skill actually leads to greater peace and confidence on a day-to-day basis. Of course, I'm still learning. I practice every day. I wish I knew of this skill years ago, but we all start from where we are.

Here is my wish for the future. I would like my work, and your work, to absorb and release the old accumulation of muck in ourselves and others.

When things come up that we don't like, we say, "I love and accept this part of me. This is my human part. I am evolving."

I would like us to bring all the hate, fear, and distrust down from our heads into our hearts and run the infinity eight loop between our thymus and heart to purify the old limiting energy. This practice is for both us and humankind. Let's pull together. Unite. Collectively add to the evolution of Earth. Let's move the human race towards greater peace, love, and joy. After all, the best is yet to come.

Chapter 7: A New World

Thank you for coming along with me on this amazing journey called Life. Let's keep walking together.

FREE OFFER FOR WRITING AMAZON REVIEW

Let me know what you think.

I would love for you to **write a review** for *Waking Up*.

As thanks, I will send you the most powerful

Tool for Waking Up:

Take it to the Heart Practice

"heart" by andhong09 | CC BY-NC-ND 2.0.

Let's make this heart practice a daily habit.

It will help you, others, and the planet to be more awake.

To receive your free Take it to the Heart Practice,

go to:

www.BarbaraBennett.net/heart

Appendix 1: State of the Union

Below is the question I ask myself. I have shared this with some friends, and they said I should include it here as an example, even though it is out of date. So, here is the question: Who, or what, am "I" at this point? Here is my journal entry.

I continue to perceive the world through a sub-conscious web of everyday ignorance, with deep imprints in my psyche from parents, school, society, and life circumstance.

- I am aware that my thoughts, feelings, and sensations are the most superficial levels of reality. When my discrimination is more subtle, I see how my understanding of "Barb" is a very old concept, which I sometimes take to be my entire self.

- I am dropping entire chunks of my identity; at the same time, my old mind keeps producing old product!

- I now realize the world is an ongoing illusory "play" in which I take part, beneath lays the present, ongoing, eternal, unchanging Moment of Life.

- I see myself as a person walking on Earth as "Barbara" with a certain constitution and personality; but I am also quite aware that this is not *fundamentally* true.

- I see how my perception is constantly changing; At times, I find myself sobbing from intense sorrow and bliss at the same time. It all just happens.

- I am all mixed up, a kaleidoscope of frequencies, a cornucopia of experiences, all projecting out through my individual, unique, bubble of perception, all occurring within infinite cosmic consciousness.

- I realize that, when I allow myself to dive deeply into my tension and discomfort, pain transforms into utter bliss.

- I take responsibility for navigating my perception/projection.

- I experience downloads of information. Flashes of knowledge come out of the blue, unbidden. When a flash of separation becomes apparent, it brings suffering; my experience of Oneness gets lost, covered up.

- I am an ongoing manifestation of spiritual energy and am beginning to learn how to function in this dense form on Earth.

- I experience Life Force unfolding, expanding, and evolving; with this, there is less and less need for the learned self. Life Force is continually morphing and revealing ground zero, Source, as It pours throughout my perception.

- I realize I am fundamentally beyond this transparent projection of form. There is no person, or personhood involved. There is no above or below, inside or outside; there is just flowing Isness doing Its thing.

- I see no polarity, no good or bad, no subject or object when at deeper levels. All is of One Agency, One Source, One flowing transmission.

- I am deeply aware of vast transparent Space, glorious black Emptiness, vibrating luminosity radiating around objects, silent sounds of manifestation, vibratory light, pixels of alive color, all projecting out as my/the world.

- I know that after physical death, there will still be Life, Awareness within a completely different environment.

- I am the whole thing! I am walking Nothingness, going in and out of various frequencies, from my usual personhood to a block of solid Reality that displays Itself instant by instant.

- I am Alive Universal Energy entering into human form to see the world through human eyes.

- I am the One Beingness. Some moments I am flowing bliss; other moments I am like a fish with a coat, encased in my old, learned, usual sense of self, which I now see as false.

- I experience how vibratory light photons, pixels of alive color, project out as my/the world.

- I sometimes experience the sense of cosmic universes, where aware beings communicate, flying among planets within an explosive, electro-magnetic, cosmic environment.

Am I crazy? No. I'm just beginning to wake up to the unlimited Reality which exists in the higher frequency dimensions. So, I'm wondering, what will happen next?

Appendix 2: Poem by My "Crazy" Aunt

What follows is a poem that my aunt wrote to her mother on Mother's Day in 1971. When you read it closely, you will see how she, as many children do, had experiences with expanded consciousness that were never noticed or acknowledged.

There Was a House in Dallas

For Mom from Joanne

There was a house in Dallas with a mother in it
And white columns and white dogs and brown boots and a swing. There was a gray knobby
Woolen cape the mother had worn as a girl.
Was I three?
I crouched on the linoleum by the gas stove, wrapped in the tent of it.
The nomad home from the day's Arabia.
I watched through the slit where the tent came together.
I saw the great columns of the mother legs glide about the kitchen.
I said, "Today I was turning a somersault on the front grass, and it came to me that someday
I was not going to BE anymore. Is that true?"
She said, "Now, Joannie, I'm trying to get supper. No. That is not true."

There was a house in Dallas with a mother in it.
She made fried chicken, potato salad, and iced tea when we went to Lake White Rock.
Was I six?

They pointed out the Masonic home looped on the alien
hill, blurred through speed
and fear and trees: Somebody old has gone there to die.
I pushed hard with my legs against the dashboard of the
Hubmobile.
Her lap was wide and warm, made of printed cotton. It had
a mother smell.
I said, "If old men go to the old men's home and old ladies
go to the old ladies' home,
Where do the old girls go?"
She said, "There are no old girls. Old girls turn into old
ladies, and old ladies go to heaven.
You're sitting on my diaphragm."

There was a house in Dallas with a mother in it. In Judy's
house, one night,
a child had a child's vision.
Was I nine?
The child broke loose, as children will, the nomad gone
over the honey suckle fence
and gone into the Self's Arabia.
I called her and she came.
She did not understand, but she took my fingers
and walked me home. She rocked me through the dark.
She sang, "This is a church," and "Ha, ha, ha."
She sang me down from those dread places, all the way
back into Dallas and her reality.
I said, "I saw God. I saw God."
She said, "Don't cry, Joannie. I'm right here."

There was a house in Dallas with a mother in it, and a
Daddy, a Clifford, an Alberta: and Rob and Roy and a
swing.
But the house grew old, as houses do,
the children gone as children are, over the honeysuckle
fence and gone into Time's Arabia.

Other children called her, other houses, and she came.
Children listen:
Were you nine? Six? Three?
She laughed again her Nana laugh; she sat on her handkerchief.
She sang those children out of those houses, all the way back into Dallas and her reality.
She rocked her generations.
She said, "This is a church, and this is a steeple: Open it up and see all the people."
She said, "Ha, ha, ha: you and me: Little Brown Jug, don't I love thee."
She said, "Don't cry, anybody; I'm right here."

Appendix 3: Further Readings

or those interested, the following is a list of books and sources that I have found useful:

A.H. Almaas – Founder of the Diamond Approach. See articles, videos, and books by and about him https://www.diamondapproach.org

Gaia www.gaia.com

Georgia Jean – Teaches and channels the Circle of Light; Jefferson Viscardi & Georgia Jean –*The Circle of Light and the Philosopher: Keys for Unlocking the Soul's Potential.* https://circleevolution.com

Jai Dev Singh – Founder of Life Force Academy. https://teachings.jaidevsingh.com

Karla McLaren -- Author of great book *The Language of Emotions: What Your Feelings Are Trying to Tell You* (Sounds True, Inc. Boulder, CO, 2010.)

Paramahansa Yogananda –*Autobiography of a Yogi* (Self-Realization Fellowship 1993)

Resonance Science Foundation contact@resonancescience.org

Russ Hudson – In 1997, along with the late Don Richard Riso, Hudson created the Enneagram Institute. https://www.Enneagraminstitute.com

Stanislav Grof –editor, Spiritual Emergency: When Personal Transformation Becomes a Crisis (G. P. Putnam's Sons NY, 1989)

Stanislav Grof & Christina Grof —*Holotropic Breathwork* (SUNY, 2010)

Suzanne Giesemann –Author and teacher on sacred mediumship.   https://www.suzannegiesemann.com

Thomas Hübl—*Healing Collective Trauma: a process for integrating our intergenerational and cultural wounds* (Sounds True, 2020) https://thomashuebl.com

Yogi Bhajan—The book that I used on my silent retreat. *I AM A WOMAN: Creative, Sacred & Invincible* (Kundalini Research Institute, 2009)

Acknowledgements

I want to thank all the people who helped make this book become a reality.

My family, especially my husband, who has loved and supported me these many years.

Jan Wheeler, who tirelessly edited transcripts, made suggestions, and supported me throughout my journey.

My readers and friends, who read drafts and gave me hours of feedback and suggestions.

Specific thanks go to the members of my 5 Around Group, Marye Gail Harrison, Fay Kandarian, Betsy Loughran and Jesse Stoner, who have listened to me and supported me for over 30 years.

Special thanks also to my inquiry partners who read drafts, gave feedback, and continue to help me dive deep on an on-going basis.

Thanks to the many people who have partnered with me during my sacred mediumship readings. They have helped me learn so much about life beyond.

Thanks to the many spiritual guides who have some forth to inform, support, and guide me in my life's journey. These same guides continue to whisper to me what, when and how to write and live.

Most of all I thank God, Source, Life Force, or whatever you prefer to call IT, for the incredible life, and opportunity, we humans are given while on Earth.

Made in the USA
Las Vegas, NV
18 August 2021